MW01233226

A 12-Month
Guide to
BETTER
PRAYER
for Women

BARBOUR BOOKS
An Imprint of Barbour Publishing, Inc.

Print ISBN 978-1-68322-297-2

eBook Editions:
Adobe Digital Edition (.epub) 978-1-68322-669-7
Kindle and MobiPocket Edition (.prc) 978-1-68322-670-3

Published by Barbour Books, an imprint of Barbour Publishing, Inc.,
1810 Barbour Drive, Uhrichsville, Ohio 44683 www.barbourbooks.com

*Our mission is to inspire the world with the life-changing message of the
Bible.*

 Member of the
Evangelical Christian
Publishers Association

Printed in the United States of America.

CONTENTS

INTRODUCTION

*The story of prayer
is the story of great achievements.*
E. M. BOUNDS

As water is to physical life, so prayer is to spiritual life. Prayer is the basic element that energizes and refreshes our spiritual life. It's not too much to say that prayer allows our spiritual life to exist—without it, we wither and crumble inside.

Though at its most basic level prayer is simply talking to God, the Bible contains many instructions and examples for improving this vital process. Over the centuries, godly men and women have studied and applied those biblical passages, explaining them in writing for the benefit of others. This little book contains some of their insights.

This *12-Month Guide to Better Prayer* features a chapter for each month of the year, drawn from the powerful writings of the following individuals:

- E. M. Bounds (1835–1913)—American minister and author of several books on prayer
- François Fénelon (1651–1715) and Madame Jeanne Guyon (1648–1717)—French theologians and writers
- Matthew Henry (1662–1714)—British clergyman and commentary writer
- Andrew Murray (1828–1917)—South African theologian and prayer expert
- Charles H. Spurgeon (1834–1892)—British preacher and writer
- R. A. Torrey (1856–1928)—American evangelist and writer
- George Whitefield (1714–1770)—British evangelist

Each entry has been lightly updated for ease of reading.

Classic Christian writings can certainly enhance your spiritual life, but should always be read in conjunction with the Bible. We suggest that you use one chapter of this book per month, reading it each day. Then, in your own copy of scripture, begin to review the verses and references in the text.

Make each chapter the basis of a monthly Bible study, and put into practice the truths you find. By year's end, your prayer life will undoubtedly be fresher, stronger, and more real than ever before.

CHAPTER 1:
Prayer—Its Possibilities
E. M. BOUNDS

*"Open your mouth wide,
and I will fill it."*
PSALM 81:10

How vast are the possibilities of prayer! How wide is its reach! What great things are accomplished by this divinely appointed means of grace! It lays its hand on Almighty God and moves Him to do what He would not otherwise do if prayer was not offered. It brings things to pass which would never otherwise occur. The story of prayer is the story of great achievements. Prayer is a wonderful power placed by Almighty God in the hands of His saints, which may be used to accomplish great purposes and to achieve unusual results. Prayer reaches to everything, takes in all things great and small which are promised by God to the children of men. The only limits to prayer are the promises of God and His ability to fulfill those promises. "Open your mouth wide, and I will fill it" (Ps. 81:10).

The records of prayer's achievements are encouraging to faith, cheering to the expectations of saints, and an inspiration to all who would pray and test its value.

Prayer is no mere untried theory. It is not some strange unique scheme, concocted in the brains of men and set on foot by them, an invention which has never been tried nor put to the test. Prayer is a divine arrangement in the moral government of God, designed for the benefit of men and intended as a means for furthering the interests of His cause on earth and carrying out His gracious purposes in redemption and providence. Prayer proves itself. It is susceptible of proving its virtue by those who pray. Prayer needs no proof other than its accomplishments.

"If anyone wills to do His will, he shall know concerning the doctrine" (John 7:17). If any man will know the virtue of prayer, if he will know what it will do, let him pray. Let him put prayer to the test.

What a breadth is given to prayer! What

heights it reaches! It is the breathing of a soul inflamed for God and inflamed for man. It goes as far as the gospel goes, and is as wide, compassionate, and prayerful as is that gospel.

How much of prayer do all these unpossessed, alienated provinces of earth demand in order to enlighten them, to impress them, and to move them toward God and His Son, Jesus Christ? Had the professed disciples of Christ only have prayed in the past as they ought to have done, the centuries would not have found these provinces still bound in death, in sin, and in ignorance.

Alas! how the unbelief of men has limited the power of God to work through prayer! What limitations have disciples of Jesus Christ put upon prayer by their prayerlessness! How the Church, with her neglect of prayer, has hedged about the gospel and shut up doors of access!

Prayer possibilities open doors for the entrance of the gospel: "meanwhile praying also for us, that God would open to us a door for the word" (Col. 4:3). Prayer opened for the apostles doors for the Word, created opportunities, and made openings to preach the gospel. The appeal by prayer was to God, because God was moved by prayer. God was thereby moved to do His own work in an enlarged way and by new ways. Prayer possibility gives not only great power, and opens doors to the gospel, but gives facility as well to the gospel. Prayer makes the gospel to go fast and to move with glorious fastness. A gospel projected by the mighty energies of prayer is neither slow, lazy, nor dull. It moves with God's power, with God's effulgence, and with angelic swiftness.

"Brethren, pray for us, that the word of the Lord may run swiftly and be glorified" (2 Thess. 3:1) is the request of the apostle Paul, whose faith reached to the possibilities of prayer for the preached Word. The gospel moves altogether too slowly, often timidly, and with feeble steps. What will make this gospel go rapidly like a race runner? What will give this gospel divine effulgence and glory, and cause it to move worthy of God and of Christ? The answer is at hand.

Prayer, more prayer, better prayer will do the deed. This means of grace will give fast going, splendor, and divinity to the gospel.

The possibilities of prayer reach to all things. Whatever concerns man's highest welfare, and whatever has to do with God's plans and purposes concerning men on earth, is a subject for prayer. In "whatever you ask" (John 14:13) is embraced all that concerns us or the children of men and God. And whatever is left out of "whatever" is left out of prayer. Where will we draw the lines which leave out or which will limit the word "whatever"? Define it, and search out and publish the things which the word does not include. If "whatever" does not include all things, then add to it the word "anything." "If you ask anything in My name, I will do it" (John 14:14).

What riches of grace, what blessings, spiritual and temporal, what good for time and eternity, would have been ours had we learned the possibilities of prayer and our faith had taken in the wide range of the divine promises to us to answer prayer! What blessings on our times and what furtherance to God's cause, had we but learned how to pray with large expectations! Who will rise up in this generation and teach the Church this lesson? It is a child's lesson in simplicity, but who has learned it well enough to put prayer to the test? It is a great lesson in its matchless and universal good. The possibilities of prayer are unspeakable, but the lesson of prayer which realizes and measures up to these possibilities, who has learned?

In His discourse in the fifteenth chapter of John, our Lord seems to connect friendship with Him to prayer, and His choosing of His disciples seems to have been with a design that through prayer they should bear much fruit. He said, "You are My friends if you do whatever I command you. . . . You did not choose Me, but I chose you and appointed you that you should go and bear fruit, and that your fruit should remain, that whatever you ask the Father in My name He may give you" (John 15:14, 16).

Here we have again the undefined and unlimited word, "whatever," as covering the rights and the things for which we are to pray in the possibilities of prayer.

We have still another declaration from Jesus: "Most assuredly, I say to you, whatever you ask the Father in My name He will give you. Until now you have asked nothing in My name. Ask, and you will receive, that your joy may be full" (John 16:23–24).

Here is a very definite exhortation from our Lord to largeness in praying. Here we are definitely urged by Him to ask for large things; announced with the dignity and solemnity indicated by the solemn phrase, "most assuredly." Why these marvelous urgencies in this last recorded and vital conversation of our Lord with His disciples? The answer is that our Lord might prepare them for the new dispensation, in which prayer was to have such marvelous results, and in which prayer was to be the chief agency to conserve and make aggressive His gospel.

In our Lord's language to His disciples about choosing them that should bear fruit, in this affluent statement of our Lord, He clearly teaches us that this matter of praying and fruit-bearing is not a petty business of our choice or a secondary matter in relation to other matters, but that He has chosen us for this very business of praying. He had specially in mind our praying, and He has chosen us of His own divine selection, and He expects us to do this one thing of praying and to do it intelligently and well.

For He before says that He had made us His friends and had brought us into bosom confidence with Him, and also into free and full conference with Him. The main object of choosing us as His disciples and of friendship with Him was that we might be the better fitted to bear the fruit of prayer.

Let us not forget that we are noting the possibilities of the true praying ones. "Anything" is the word of area and circumference. How far it reaches we may not know. How wide it spreads, our minds fail to discover. What is there which is not within its reach? Why does Jesus repeat and exhaust these words, all-inclusive and boundless words, if He does not desire to emphasize the unbounded magnificence and illimitable munificence of prayer? Why does He press men to pray, so that our very poverty might be enriched and our limitless inheritance by prayer be secured?

We affirm with absolute certainty that Almighty God answers prayer. The vast possibilities and the urgent necessity of prayer lie in this stupendous fact that God hears and answers prayer. And God hears and answers all prayer. He hears and answers every prayer, where the true conditions of praying are met. Either this is so or it is not. If not, then there is nothing in prayer. Then prayer is but the recitation of words, a mere verbal performance, an empty ceremony. Then prayer is an altogether useless exercise.

But if what we have said is true, then there are vast possibilities in prayer. Then is it far-reaching in its scope, and wide is its range. Then is it true that prayer can lay its hand upon Almighty God and move Him to do great and wonderful things.

The benefits, the possibilities, and the necessity of prayer are not merely subjective but are peculiarly objective in their character. Prayer aims at a definite object. Prayer has a direct design in view.

Prayer always has something specific before the mind's eye. There may be some subjective benefits which accrue from praying, but this is altogether secondary and incidental.

Prayer always drives directly at an object and seeks to secure a desired end. Prayer is asking, seeking, and knocking at a door for something we have not, which we desire, and which God has promised to us.

Prayer is a direct address to God. "In everything. . .let your requests be made known to God" (Phil. 4:6). Prayer secures blessings and makes men better because it reaches the ear of God. Prayer is only for the betterment of men when it has affected God and moved Him to do something for men. Prayer affects men by affecting God.

Prayer moves men because it moves God to move men. Prayer influences men by influencing God to influence them. Prayer moves the hand that moves the world.

That power is prayer, which soars on high,
Through Jesus to the throne;
And moves the hand which moves the world,
To bring salvation down.

The utmost possibilities of prayer have rarely been realized. The promises of God are so great to those who truly pray, when He puts Himself so fully into the hands of the praying ones, that it almost staggers our faith and causes us to hesitate with astonishment. His promise to answer, and to do and to give "all things," "anything," "whatever," and "all things whatsoever," is so large, so great, so exceedingly broad, that we stand back in amazement and give ourselves to questioning and doubt. We "[waver] at the promises through unbelief." Really, the promises of God to prayer have been pared down by us to our little faith and have been brought down to the low level of our narrow notions about God's ability, liberality, and resources. Let us ever keep in mind and never for one moment allow ourselves to doubt the statement that God means what He says in all of His promises. God's promises are His own word. His veracity is at stake in them. To question them is to doubt His veracity. He cannot afford to prove faithless to His word. "In hope of eternal life which God, who cannot lie, promised before time began" (Titus 1:2). His promises are for plain people, and He means to do for all who pray just what He says He will do—"for He who promised is faithful" (Heb. 10:23).

Unfortunately, we have failed to lay ourselves out in praying. We have limited the

Holy One of Israel. The ability to pray can be secured by the grace and power of the Holy Spirit, but it demands so strenuous and high a character that it is a rare thing for a man or woman to be on praying ground and on pleading terms with God. It is as true today as it was in the days of Elijah that "the effective, fervent prayer of a righteous man avails much" (James 5:16). How much such a prayer avails, who can tell?

The possibilities of prayer are the possibilities of faith. Prayer and faith are Siamese twins. One heart animates them both. Faith is always praying. Prayer is always believing. Faith must have a tongue by which it can speak. Prayer is the tongue of faith. Faith must receive. Prayer is the hand of faith stretched out to receive. Prayer must rise and soar. Faith must give prayer the wings to fly and soar. Prayer must have an audience with God. Faith opens the door, and access and audience are given. Prayer asks. Faith lays its hand on the thing asked for.

God's omnipotent power is the basis of omnipotent faith and omnipotent praying. "All things are possible to him who believes" (Mark

9:23), and "whatever things you ask" (Matt. 21:22) are given to him who prays. God's decree and death yield readily to Hezekiah's faith and prayer. When God's promise and man's praying are united by faith, then nothing shall be impossible. Importunate prayer is so all-powerful and irresistible that it obtains promises, or wins where the prospect and the promise seem to be against it. In fact, the New Testament promise includes all things in heaven and in earth. God, by promise, puts all things He possesses into man's hands. Prayer and faith put man in possession of this boundless inheritance.

Prayer is not an indifferent or a small thing. It is not a sweet little privilege. It is a great prerogative, far-reaching in its effects. Failure to pray entails losses far beyond the person who neglects it. Prayer is not a mere episode of the Christian life. Rather, the whole of life is a preparation for and the result of prayer. In its condition, prayer is the sum of religion. Faith is but a channel of prayer. Faith gives it wings and swiftness. Prayer is the lungs through which holiness breathes. Prayer is not only the language of spiritual life, but makes its very essence and forms its real character.

> O for a faith that will not shrink
> Though pressed by every foe;
> That will not tremble on the brink
> Of any earthly woe.
>
> Lord, give us such a faith as this,
> And then, whate'er may come,
> We'll taste e'en here, the hallowed bliss
> Of our eternal home.

Lord God, the story of prayer might be the story of great achievements, but my personal journey reads more like a survival tale, lurching from one day's emergency to the next. Not everyone can be like Esther, who fasted, prayed, and wrested victory for her people from the hands of her enemy. I'm more like Hannah, who asked You for a son, and the Phoenician woman who beseeched Jesus to heal her child. I may not be like Lydia who offered her house as a place of worship, but I have often wept before You, like the woman who wiped Jesus' feet with her tears. As I rehearse Your gracious response to my prayers, open my eyes to the grandeur of Your achievements in my life. Amen.

Our Father, Your Kingdom come, Your will be done. If prayer is to be the currency in Your Kingdom that I can spend to see Your will accomplished, then teach me to invest it intelligently and well. School me in Your Word and Your promises that I may know what I may claim without reservation or hesitation. Open my eyes to the limitless possibilities prayers afford me. Expand my vision to see my home as Your castle, my job as Your marketplace, my pain as an opportunity to watch You work. Explode my prayers for me in the now, to the ends of the earth and beyond, throughout eternity. Paint my prayers with the colors of heaven. Amen.

Loving Father, You long to give generously to Your children. Forgive me when I push away Your gifts by refusing to claim them in prayer. I complain I am in want, when I have not relied on Your supply. I lament I am weak and helpless, when I haven't asked for Your strength. I wander without direction without looking to You to lead me in the way I should go. I hold back from asking too much, when instead I miss the mark by asking for too little. Show me where to boldly go in prayer. Forgive me, O God of Salvation, when I hinder Your work among the nations by my failure to pray for the furtherance of Your Kingdom. May You find me faithful in prayer. Amen.

Redeemer God, You sent Your Son to die so that all the world might be saved. Make it so, Lord. I praise You that through prayer I have a part *in reaching people in the farthest reaches of Mongolia with the Gospel, to those without any of the electronic devices we count on to keep in touch with the world. I pray for my Jerusalem, my family, my town. My Judea—my state, my country. And I pray for the spread of the Gospel to every person on earth. Show me specific people and language groups who have not yet heard the good news, that I may pray for them. Make me a world citizen, praying for the everyday people behind news reports. Expand the walls of my heart to include people I have never even heard of in my prayers. In Jesus' name, Amen.*

CHAPTER 2:
The Secret of Power in Prayer, Part 1
CHARLES H. SPURGEON

*"If you abide in Me, and My words
abide in you, you will ask what
you desire, and it shall
be done for you."*
JOHN 15:7

Believers do not enjoy the gifts of divine grace all at once. Coming to Christ, we are saved by a true union with Him. But it is by *abiding* in that union that we further receive the purity, the joy, the power, and the blessedness that are stored up in Him for His people. See how our Lord states this when He speaks to the believing Jews in the eighth chapter of this gospel: "If you abide in My word, you are My disciples indeed. And you shall know the truth, and the truth shall make you free" (John 8:31–32). We do not know all the truth of God at once; we learn it by *abiding* in Jesus.

Perseverance in divine grace is an educational process by which we learn the truth of God fully. The emancipating power of that truth is also gradually perceived and enjoyed. The truth will make you free; one bond after another snaps, and we are free indeed. You who are young beginners in the divine life may be cheered to know that there is something better, still, for you—you have not yet received the full recompense of your faith. As our hymn puts it, "It is better than before." You will have happier views of heavenly things as you climb the hill of spiritual experience.

As you abide in Christ, you will have firmer confidence, richer joy, greater stability, more communion with Jesus, and greater delight in the Lord your God.

Infancy is beset with many evils from which manhood is exempt—it is the same in the spiritual as in the natural world.

There are these degrees of attainment among believers, and the Savior here incites us to reach a high position by mentioning a certain privilege that is not for all who say that they are in Christ but for those only who are *abiders* in Him. Every believer should be an abider, but many have hardly earned the name as yet. Jesus says, "If you abide in Me, and My words abide in you, you will ask what you desire, and it shall be done for you" (John 15:7). You have to *live* with Christ to know Him, and the longer you live with Him, the more you will admire and adore Him, and the more you will receive from Him, even grace for grace.

Truly He is a blessed Christ to one who is but a month old in divine grace. But these babes can hardly tell what a precious Jesus He is to those whose acquaintance with Him covers well near half a century! Jesus, in the esteem of abiding believers, grows sweeter and dearer, fairer and lovelier each day. Not that He improves in Himself, for He is perfect. But as *we* increase in our knowledge of Him, we appreciate more thoroughly His matchless excellences.

How glowingly do His old acquaintances exclaim, "Yes, He is altogether lovely!" Oh, that we may continue to grow up in Him in all things who is our head, that we thus may prize Him more and more!

I call your earnest attention to our text,

begging you to consider with me three questions. First, what is this special blessing? "You will ask what you desire, and it shall be done for you." Secondly, how is this special blessing obtained? "If you abide in Me, and My words abide in you." Then, thirdly, why is it obtained in this way? There must be a reason for the conditions laid down as necessary to obtaining the promised power in prayer.

Oh, that the anointing of the Holy Spirit that abides in us may now make this subject very profitable to us!

What is this special blessing? Let us read the verse again. Jesus says, "If you abide in Me, and My words abide in you, you will ask what you desire, and it shall be done for you."

Observe that our Lord had been warning us that, severed from Him, we can do nothing, and therefore we might naturally have expected that He would now show us how we can do all spiritual acts.

But the text does not run as we should have expected it to run. The Lord Jesus does not say, "Without Me you can do nothing, but if you abide in Me and My words abide in you, you will do all spiritual and gracious things."

He does not now speak of what they should, *themselves,* be enabled to do but of what should be done for them.

He says not, "Strength will be given you sufficient for all those holy doings of which you are incapable apart from Me." That would have been true enough, and it is the truth of God that we looked for here. But our most wise Lord improves upon all parallelisms of speech and improves upon all expectancies of heart and says something better still. He does not say, "If you abide in Me and My words abide in you, you will do spiritual things." But, *"you will ask."* By prayer you will be enabled to do. But before all attempts to do, you will ask. The choice privilege here given is a mighty prevailing *prayerfulness.* Power in prayer is very much the gauge of our spiritual condition. And when that is secured to us in a high degree, we are favored as to all other matters.

One of the first results, then, of our abiding union with Christ will be the certain exercise of prayer. You will ask. If others neither seek, nor knock, nor ask, you, at any rate, will do so. Those who keep away from Jesus do not pray. Those in whom communion with Christ is suspended feel as if they could not pray. But Jesus says, "If you abide in Me, and My words abide in you, you will ask." Prayer comes spontaneously from those who abide in Jesus, even as certain oriental trees, without pressure, shed their fragrant gums.

Prayer is the natural out-gushing of a soul in communion with Jesus. Just as the leaf and the fruit will come out of the vine without any conscious effort on the part of the branch but simply because of its living union with the stem, so prayer buds and blossoms and produces fruit out of souls abiding in Jesus. As stars shine, so do abiders pray. It is their use and their second nature. They do not say to themselves, "Now it is the time for us to get to our task and pray." No, they pray as wise men eat, namely, when the desire for it is upon them. They do not cry out as under bondage, "At this time I ought to be in prayer but I do not feel like it. What a weariness it is!" No, they have a glad errand at the mercy seat and they are rejoiced to go upon it.

Hearts abiding in Christ send forth

supplications as fires send out flames and sparks. Souls abiding in Jesus open the day with prayer. Prayer surrounds them as an atmosphere all day long. At night they fall asleep praying. I have known them even to dream a prayer and, at any rate, they are able joyfully to say, "When I awake, I am still with You" (Ps. 139:18). Habitual asking comes out of abiding in Christ. You will not need urging to prayer when you are abiding with Jesus. He says you will ask. And depend upon it, you will!

You will also feel most powerfully the *necessity* of prayer. Your great need of prayer will be vividly seen. Do I hear you say, "What? When we abide in Christ and His words abide in us, have we not already attained?" Far are we, then, from being satisfied with ourselves. It is *then* that we feel more than ever that we must ask for *more* divine grace. He that knows Christ best knows his own necessities best.

He that is most conscious of life in Christ is also most convinced of his own death apart from Christ. He who most clearly discerns the perfect character of Jesus will be most urgent in prayer for divine grace to grow like He. The more I seem to be in my Lord, the more I desire to obtain from Him, since I know that all that is in Him is put there on purpose that I may receive it.

"Of His fullness we have all received, and grace for grace" (John 1:16). It is just in proportion as we are linked to Christ's fullness that we feel the necessity of drawing from it by constant prayer.

Nobody needs to prove to an abider in Christ the doctrine of prayer, for we enjoy the thing itself. Prayer is now as much a necessity of our spiritual life as breath is of our natural life—we cannot live without asking favors of the Lord! "If you abide in Me, and My words abide in you, you will ask"—and you will not wish to cease from asking. He has said, "Seek My face," and your heart will answer, "Your face, LORD, I will seek" (Ps. 27:8).

Note next, that the fruit of our abiding is not only the exercise of prayer and a sense of the necessity of prayer, but it includes *liberty* in prayer. "You will ask what you desire." Have you not been on your knees at times without power to pray? Have you not felt that you could not plead as you desired? You wanted to pray but the waters were frozen up and would not flow. You said mournfully, "I am shut up, and I cannot get out" (Ps. 88:8). The will was present but not the freedom to present that will in prayer. Do you, then, desire liberty in prayer so that you may speak with God as a man speaks with his friend? Here is the way to it, "If you abide in Me, and My words abide in you, you will ask what you desire."

I do not mean that you will gain liberty as to mere fluency of utterance—for that is a very *inferior* gift. Fluency is a questionable endowment, especially when it is not attended with weight of thought and depth of feeling. Some brethren pray by the yard.

But true prayer is measured by weight and not by length. A single groan before God may have more fullness of prayer in it than a fine oration of great length. He that dwells with God in Christ Jesus is the man whose steps are enlarged in intercession.

He comes boldly because he abides at the throne. He sees the golden scepter stretched out and hears the King saying, "Ask what you will and it will be done to you."

It is the man who abides in conscious union with his Lord who has freedom of access in prayer. Well may he come to Christ readily, for he is in Christ, and abides in Him. Attempt not to seize this holy liberty by excitement, or presumption—there is but one way of really gaining it and here it is—"If you abide in Me, and My words abide in you, you will ask what you desire." By this means alone will you be enabled to open your mouth wide, that God may fill it. Thus will you become Israel's children, and as princes, have power with God.

This is not all. The favored man has the privilege of successful prayer. "You will ask what you desire, and it shall be done for you." You may not do it, but it will be done to you. You long to bear fruit. Ask and it will be done to you. Look at the vine branch. It simply remains in the vine, and by remaining in the vine, the fruit comes from it. It is done to it. Brothers and sisters in Christ, the purpose of your being, its one object and design, is to bring forth fruit to the glory of the Father. To gain this end you must abide in Christ, as the branch abides in the vine. This is the method by which your prayer for fruitfulness will become successful. "It shall be done for you."

Concerning this matter, "you will ask what you desire, and it shall be done for you." You will have wonderful prevalence with God in prayer, insomuch that before you call, He will answer, and while you are yet speaking, He will hear. "The desire of the righteous will be granted" (Prov. 10:24). To the same effect is the other text: "Delight yourself also in the LORD, and He shall give you the desires of your heart" (Ps. 37:4). There is a great breadth in this text, "You will ask what you desire, and it shall be done for you." The Lord gives the abider carte blanche. He puts into his hand a signed check and permits him to fill it up as he wills.

Does the text mean what it says? I never knew my Lord to say anything He did not mean. I am sure that He may sometimes mean more than we understand Him to say, but He never means less. Mind you, He does not say to all men, "I will give you whatever you ask." Oh no, that would be an unkind kindness— but He speaks to His disciples and says, "If you abide in Me, and My words abide in you, you will ask what you desire, and it shall be done for you." It is to a certain class of men who have already received great grace at His hands.

It is to them He commits this marvelous power of prayer.

O my dear friends, if I may covet earnestly one thing above every other, it is that I may be able to ask what I will of the Lord and have it! The man who prevails in prayer is the man to preach successfully, for he may well prevail with man for God when he has already prevailed with God for men! This is the man to face the difficulties of business life. For what can baffle him when he can take all to God in prayer? One such man as this, or one such woman as this in a church is worth ten thousand of us common people. In these we find the peerage of the skies. In these are the men in whom is fulfilled God's purpose concerning man, whom He made to have dominion over all the works of His hands.

The stamp of sovereignty is on the brows of these men. They shape the history of nations, they guide the current events through their power on high. We see Jesus with all things put under Him by the divine purpose, and as we rise into that image, we also are clothed with dominion and are made kings and priests to God.

Behold Elijah, with the keys of the rain swinging at his girdle, he shuts or opens the windows of heaven! There are such men still alive. Aspire to be such men and women, I beseech you, that to you the text may be fulfilled, "You will ask what you desire, and it shall be done for you."

The text seems to imply that if we reach this point of privilege, this gift will be a perpetuity. "You will ask," you will always ask; you will never get beyond asking, but you will ask successfully. "You will ask what you desire, and it shall be done for you." Here we have the gift of *continual* prayer.

Not for the week of prayer, not during a month's conference, nor upon a few special occasions will you pray prevailingly. But you will possess this power with God so long as you abide in Christ and His words abide in you. God will put His omnipotence at your disposal. He will put forth His Godhead to fulfill the desires that His own Spirit has worked in you.

I wish I could make this jewel glitter before the eyes of all the saints till they cried out, "Oh, that we had it!" This power in prayer is like the sword of Goliath. Wisely may every David say, "There is none like it; give it to me" (1 Sam. 21:9). This weapon of all-prayer beats the enemy and at the same time enriches its possessor with all the wealth of God. How can he lack anything to whom the Lord has said, "Ask what you will, and it will be done to you"? Oh come, let us seek this promise. Listen and learn the way. Follow me, while by the light of the text I point out the path. May the Lord lead us in it by His Holy Spirit!

Life-giving vine, I bow in awe that You have chosen me as one of Your branches. You grafted me, a Gentile by birth, onto Israel's branch, that I may enjoy the fatness, the amazing abundance, available through Your vine (Romans 11:17–18). You performed the operation that I may enjoy the benefits of Your life-giving sap and bear holy fruit. Teach me to tend to the graft site, to keep it healthy. Daily may I seek Your cleansing for sins of omission and commission. Teach me to swim in Your life-giving water, that I may know You better and better. The more of You I learn, the more I turn to prayer. When I stop growing, I start dying. The earthly proverb speaks a spiritual truth. And oh, the glory that I will spend eternity ever knowing more and more of the infinite God. In Jesus' name, amen.

Father, I confess I find the command to "pray without ceasing" daunting. Life isn't lived on our knees or in a secluded place. I can't close my eyes when I'm driving or stop in the middle of a business call to whisper a prayer. I get that I should cultivate an attitude of prayer, but what does that look like? Perhaps I should take my cue from David, who discovered he couldn't escape Your Spirit. And Paul, who knew from experience that nothing could ever separate him from Your love. Make me conscious of Your everywhere-ness, that we may walk hand-in-hand. May prayer be both my habitual response and also my disciplined plan of action, that I might pray until the answer is received. For Your glory and in Jesus' name, Amen.

Abba Father, You have invited me, even commanded me, to come boldly before Your throne of grace. Forgive me when I bring You safe prayers—when I add the caveat "if it be Your will" when claiming one of Your promises. Rather, make me bold like Esther, who petitioned the king at the risk of her life. Make me as confident as a rightful daughter asking her father to pick her up and hold her close. To You, I will always be a toddler, welcome to sit on Your lap and ask You for gifts. Make my heart like a little child when I pray. Teach me the liberty of praying according to Your promises, for then I can know I pray aright. Amen.

Giving God, how can I thank You enough for unprayed-for-answers? How gracious, how amazing, that You respond to my need before I am aware of it. When I pray today for my friend's need yesterday, I do so, trusting You heard my prayer and answered it even in my tardiness. Forgive me that laxness, Lord. Teach me the discipline of praying in a timely manner. Let me rest in Your peace, knowing nothing that happens to me today will catch You by surprise, whether it's my child's accident, bad feelings with a neighbor, a new responsibility dumped in my lap, or any of the things that happen on any given day. As I abide in You more and more, open my eyes to Your activity on my behalf. Amen.

CHAPTER 3:
The Secret of Power in Prayer, Part 2
CHARLES H. SPURGEON

*"If you abide in Me, and My words
abide in you, you will ask what
you desire, and it shall
be done for you."*
JOHN 15:7

How is this privilege of mighty prayer-fulness *to be obtained*? The answer is, "If you abide in Me, and My words abide in you." Here are the two feet by which we climb to power with God in prayer.

Beloved, the first line tells us that we are to abide in Christ Jesus our Lord. It is taken for granted that we are already in Him. May it be taken for granted in your case, dear hearer? If so, you are to abide where you are. As believers we are to remain tenaciously clinging to Jesus, lovingly knit to Jesus. We are to abide in Him by always trusting Him, and Him only, with the same simple faith that joined us to Him at the first. We must never admit any other thing or person into our heart's confidence as our hope of salvation. We must rest alone in Jesus as we received Him at the first.

His Godhead, His manhood, His life, His death, His resurrection, and His glory at the right hand of the Father—in a word, Himself—must be our heart's sole reliance.

This is absolutely essential. A temporary faith will not save. An abiding faith is necessary.

But abiding in the Lord Jesus does not only mean *trusting* in Him. It includes our yielding ourselves up to Him to receive His life and to let that life work out its results in us. We live *in* Him, *by* Him, *for* Him, *to* Him, when we abide in Him. We feel that all our separate life has gone, for "you died, and your life is hidden with Christ" (Col. 3:3). We are nothing if we get away from Jesus. Then we would be branches withered and only fit to be cast into the fire. We have no reason for existence except that which we find in Christ, and what a marvelous reason that is! The vine needs the branch as truly as the branch needs the vine. No vine ever bore any fruit except upon its branches. Truly it bears all the branches and so bears all the fruit.

But yet it is by the branch that the vine displays its fruitfulness. Thus are abiding believers necessary to the fulfillment of their Lord's design. Wonderful thing to say, that the saints are necessary to their Savior! The church is His body, the fullness of Him that fills all in all. I want you to recognize this: that you may see your blessed responsibility, your practical obligation to bring forth fruit that the Lord Jesus may be glorified in you.

Abide in Him and never diminish your consecration to His honor and glory, never dream of being your own master. Be not the servant of men but abide in Christ. Let Him be the object, as well as the Source, of your existence.

Oh, if you get there and stop there in perpetual communion with your Lord, you will soon realize a joy, a delight, a power in prayer such as you never knew before! There are times when we are conscious that we are in Christ and we know our fellowship with Him. And oh, the joy and the peace that we drink from this cup! Let us abide there. "Abide in Me," says Jesus.

You are not to come and go but to *abide*. Let that blessed sinking of yourself into His life, the spending of all your powers for Jesus, and the firm faith of your union with Him remain in you forever. Oh, that we might attain to this by the Holy Spirit!

As if to help us to understand this, our gracious Lord has given us a delightful parable. Let us look through this discourse of the vine and its branches. Jesus says, "Every branch in Me that. . .bears fruit He prunes" (John 15:2). Take care that you abide in Christ when you are being purged. "Oh," says one, "I thought I was a Christian. But, alas! I have more troubles than ever. Men ridicule me, the devil tempts me, and my business affairs go wrong." Brother, if you are to have *power* in prayer, you must take care that you abide in Christ when the sharp knife is cutting everything away.

Endure trial and never dream of giving up your faith because of it.

Say, "Though He slay me, yet will I trust Him" (Job 13:15).

Your Lord warned you when you first came into the vine that you would have to be purged and cut closely. And if you are now feeling the purging process, you must not think that some strange thing has happened to you. Rebel not because of anything you may have to suffer from the dear hand of your heavenly Father who is the husbandman of the vineyard. Rather, cling to Jesus all the more closely. Say, "Cut, Lord, cut to the quick if You will! But I will cling to You. To whom should we go? You have the words of eternal life."

Yes, cling to Jesus when the purging knife is in His hand, and so shall you "ask what you desire, and it shall be done for you."

Take care, also, that when the purging operation has been carried out, you still cleave to your Lord. Notice the third and fourth verses of John 15: "You are already clean because of the word which I have spoken to you. Abide in Me, and I in you." Abide after cleansing where you were before cleansing. When you are sanctified, abide where you were when first justified. When you see the work of the Spirit increasing in you, do not let the devil tempt. He will try to get you to boast that now you are somebody, you need not come to Jesus as a poor sinner and rest in His precious blood alone for salvation. Abide still in Jesus. As you kept to Him when the knife cut you, keep to Him now that the tender grapes begin to form.

Do not say to yourself, "What a fruitful branch I am! How greatly I adorn the vine! Now I am full of vigor!" You are nothing and nobody. Only as you abide in Christ are you one whit better than the waste wood that is burned in the fire. "But do we not make progress?" Yes, we grow, but we abide. We never go an inch further. We abide in Him. Or, if not, we are cast forth and are withered. Our whole hope lies in Jesus at our best times as well as at our worst. Jesus says, "You are already clean because of the word which I have spoken to you. Abide in Me, and I in you." Abide in Him as to all your fruitfulness. "As the branch cannot bear fruit of itself, unless it abides in the vine, neither can you, unless you abide in Me" (John 15:4).

"Here, then, I have something to do," cries one. Certainly you have, but not apart from Jesus. The branch has to bear fruit. But if the branch imagines that it is going to produce a cluster, or even a grape out of itself alone, it is utterly mistaken. The fruit of the branch must come forth of the stem.

Your work for Christ must be Christ's work in you or else it will be good for nothing. I pray you, see to this. Your Sunday school teaching, your preaching, or whatever you do, must be done in Christ Jesus. Not by your natural talent can you win souls, nor by plans of your own inventing can you save men. Beware of homemade schemes. Do for Jesus what Jesus bids you do. Remember that our work for Christ, as we call it, must be Christ's work first if it is to be accepted of Him. Abide in Him as to your fruit bearing.

Yes, abide in Him as to your very life. Do not say, "I have been a Christian now twenty or thirty years; I can do without continued dependence upon Christ." No, you could not do without Him if you were as old as Methuselah! Your very *being* as a Christian depends upon your still clinging, still trusting, still depending on your Master, and this He must give you, for it all comes from Him and Him alone.

To sum it all up, if you want that splendid

power in prayer of which I spoke just now, you must remain in loving, living, lasting, conscious, practical, abiding union with the Lord Jesus Christ. And if you get to that by divine grace, then you will ask what you desire and it will be done to you.

But there is a second qualification mentioned in the text, and you must not forget it: "and My words abide in you." How important, then, are Christ's words! He said in the fourth verse, "Abide in me and I in you," and now as a parallel to this it is, "If you abide in Me, and My words abide in you." What, then? Are Christ's words and Himself identical? Yes, practically so.

Some talk about Christ being the Master, but as to doctrine they do not care what His Word declares. So long as their hearts are right toward His person, they claim liberty of thought. Yes, but this is a mere subterfuge.

We cannot separate Christ from the Word. For, in the first place, He *is* the Word. And, in the next place, how dare we call Him Master and Lord and do not the things that He says and reject the truth of God that He teaches?

We must obey His precepts or He will not accept us as disciples. Especially that precept of love that is the essence of all His words. We must love God and our brethren—yes, we must cherish love to all men and seek their good. Anger and malice must be far from us. We must walk even as He walked. If Christ's words abide not in you, both as to belief and practice, you are not in Christ.

Christ and His gospel and His commands are one.

If you will not have Christ and His words, neither will He have you nor your words, and you will ask in vain. You will by-and-by give up asking; you will become as a withered branch. Beloved, I am persuaded better things of you and things that accompany salvation, though I thus speak.

Oh, for divine grace to pass through these two-leaved gates, these two golden doors! "If you abide in Me, and My words abide in you." Push through the two and enter into this large room: "You will ask what you desire, and it shall be done for you."

Lord Jesus, You have called me to abide in You. Your promise to give me whatever I ask rests on that abiding. But I am a restless creature, prone to wander. Tether me to You. When the worries of life or the cries of a child wake me at night, remind me that every breath comes from You. As I move from bed to crib to office, may I be aware of Your company in every step I take. Any good I do comes from You. Apart from You, I will quickly grow weary. Make me thirsty for the sweet sap of Your vine. In every beat of the rhythms of my life, make me aware of Your life pumping through me, until I know everything in Jesus, and Jesus everything. Amen.

Divine gardener, my mind understands You are responsible for the health of the vine and its branches. But when it comes to the actual process, I don't like seeing the doctor. When You approach me with pruning shears in hand, I want to hide. But there is nowhere I can go to where You can't find me. Cultivate in me a spirit of gratitude for the pruning that prepares me for new growth. Keep me from doubt during those dark times.

Like Job, let me say, "Though He slay me, yet will I trust Him" (Job 13:15). When you strip me of prized fruit that I may have valued more than the Giver, forgive me. Turn my eyes to the new growth and opportunities that lie ahead. In and through and for Jesus, amen.

Lord God Almighty, all things were made by You. You display Your glory in the heavens—and still in the midst of all that grandeur, You formed me in my mother's womb and have chosen to give me life. Everything I have and am is because of You. Yet when You have chosen to use me in some work, great or small, I may choose to boast. I may claim my children's success as my own. I may speak as though a spiritual insight or answered prayer happened within my power. Oh, forgive my arrogance, Lord! If I must boast, let me boast in my infirmities, for Your strength is made perfect in them. In Jesus' name, amen.

Author God, speak to my heart in Your written Word and by the Holy Spirit. May the same Spirit that moved the writers of scripture breathe life into them as I read, study, meditate, and memorize. And I confess I don't spend enough time in Your Word. Sometimes I exchange Your

Word for books about Your Word, neglecting Your direct message to me and choosing instead what someone else says about it. Forgive me, too, when I am satisfied with head-learning without allowing it to permeate into every area of my life. Make me a doer and not only a hearer, lest I deceive myself. Amen.

CHAPTER 4:
On Prayer and the Principal Exercises of Piety
FRANÇOIS FÉNELON AND
MADAME JEANNE GUYON

We do not know what we should pray for as we ought, but the Spirit Himself makes intercession for us with groanings which cannot be uttered.
ROMANS 8:26

True prayer is only another name for the love of God. Its excellence does not consist in the multitude of our words; for our Father knows what things we have need of before we ask Him. The true prayer is that of the heart, and the heart prays only for what it desires. To pray, then, is to desire—but to desire what God would have us desire. He who asks what he does not from the bottom of his heart desire, is mistaken in thinking that he prays. Let him spend days in reciting prayers, in meditation, or in inciting himself to pious exercises—he prays not once truly, if he really doesn't desire the things he pretends to ask.

How few there are who pray—for how few are they who desire what is truly good! Crosses, external and internal humiliation, renouncement of our own wills, the death of self, and the establishment of God's throne upon the ruins of self-love—these are indeed good; not to desire these, is not to pray; to desire them seriously, soberly, constantly, and with reference to all the details of life, this is true prayer; not to desire them, and yet to suppose we pray, is an illusion like that of the wretched who dream themselves happy. Alas! how many souls full of self, and of an imaginary desire for perfection in the midst of hosts of voluntary imperfections, have never yet uttered this true prayer of the heart! It is in reference to this that Saint Augustine says: "He that loveth little, prayeth little; he that loveth much prayeth much."

On the other hand, that heart in which the true love of God and true desire exist never ceases to pray. Love, hidden in the bottom of the soul, prays without ceasing, even when the mind is drawn another way. God continually beholds the desire which He has Himself implanted in the soul, though it may at times be unconscious of its existence; His heart is touched by it; it ceaselessly attracts His mercies; it is that Spirit which, according to St. Paul, helps our infirmities and "makes intercession for us with groanings which cannot be uttered" (Rom. 8:26).

Love desires of God that He would give us what we need and that He would have less regard to our frailty than to the purity of our intentions. It even covers over our trifling defects and purifies us like a consuming fire: "He makes intercession for the saints according to the will of God" (Rom. 8:27). For "we do not know what we should pray for as we ought" (Rom. 8:26) and, in our ignorance, frequently request what would be injurious; we should like fervor of devotion, distinct sensible joys, and apparent perfections, which would serve to nourish within us the life of self and a confidence in our own strength; but love leads us on, abandons us to all the operations of grace, puts us entirely at the disposal of God's will, and thus prepares us for all His secret designs.

Then we will all things and yet nothing. What God gives is precisely what we should have desired to ask; for we will whatever He wills and only that. Thus, this state contains all prayer: it is a work of the heart which includes all desire. The Spirit prays within us for those very things which the Spirit Himself wills to give us.

Even when we are occupied with outward things, and our thoughts drawn off by the providential engagements of our position, we still carry within us a constantly burning fire, which not only cannot be extinguished but nourishes a secret prayer, and is like a lamp continually lighted before the throne of God, "I sleep, but my heart is awake" (Song of Sol. 5:2). "Blessed are those servants whom the master, when he comes, will find watching" (Luke 12:37).

There are two principal points of attention necessary for the preservation of this constant spirit of prayer which unites us with God: We must continually seek to cherish it, and we must avoid everything that tends to make us lose it.

In order to cherish it, we should pursue a regulated course of reading; we must have appointed seasons of secret prayer, and frequent states of recollection during the day; we should make use of retirement when we feel the need of it, or when it is advised by those of greater experience, and unite in the ordinances appropriate to our condition.

We should greatly fear and be exceedingly cautious to avoid all things that have a tendency to make us lose this state of prayer. Thus we should decline those worldly occupations and associates which dissipate the mind, pleasures which excite the passions, and everything calculated to awaken the love of the world and those old inclinations that have caused us so much trouble.

There is an infinity of detail in these two heads; general directions only can be given, because each individual case presents features peculiar to itself.

We should choose those works for reading which instruct us in our duty and in our faults; which, while they point out the greatness of God, teach us what is our duty to Him, and how very far we are from performing it; not those barren productions which melt and sentimentalize the heart; *the tree must bear fruit*; we can only judge of the life of the root by its fecundity.

The first effect of a sincere love is an earnest desire to know all that we ought to do to gratify the object of our affection.

Any other desire is a proof that we love ourselves under a pretense of loving God; that we are seeking an empty and deceitful consolation in Him; that we would use God as an instrument for our pleasure, instead of sacrificing that for His glory. God forbid that His children should so love Him! Cost what it may, we must both know and do without reservation what He requires of us.

Seasons of secret prayer must be regulated by the leisure, the disposition, the condition, and the inward impulse of each individual.

Meditation is not prayer, but it is its necessary foundation; it brings to mind the truths which God has revealed. We should be conversant not only with all the mysteries of Jesus Christ, and the truths of His gospel, but also with everything they ought to operate in us for our regeneration; we should be colored and penetrated by them as wool is by the dye.

So familiar should they become to us, that, in consequence of seeing them at all times and ever near to us, we may acquire the habit of forming no judgment except in their light; that they may be to us our only guide in matters of practice, as the rays of the sun are our only light in matters of perception.

When these truths are once, as it were, incorporated in us, then it is that our praying begins to be real and fruitful. Up to that point it was but the shadow; we thought we had penetrated to the inmost recesses of the gospel, when we had barely set foot upon the vestibule—all our most tender and lively feelings, all our firmest resolutions, all our clearest and farthest views, were but the rough and shapeless mass from which God would hew in us His likeness.

When His celestial rays begin to shine within us, then we see in the true light; then there is no truth to which we do not instantaneously assent, as we admit, without any process of reasoning, the splendor of the sun, the moment we behold His rising beams. Our union with God must be the result of our faithfulness in doing and suffering all His will.

Our meditations should become every day deeper and more interior. I say *deeper*, because by frequent and humble meditation upon

God's truth, we penetrate further and further in search of new treasures; and *more interior,* because as we sink more and more to enter into these truths, they also descend to penetrate the very substance of our souls. Then it is that a simple word goes further than whole sermons.

The very things which had been fruitlessly and coldly heard a hundred times before, now nourish the soul with a hidden manna, having an infinite variety of flavors for days in succession. Let us beware, too, of ceasing to meditate upon truths which have heretofore been blessed to us, so long as there remains any nourishment in them, so long as they yet yield us anything; it is a certain sign that we still need their ministration; we derive instruction from them without receiving any precise or distinct impression; there is an indescribable something in them, which helps us more than all our reasonings. We behold a truth, we love it and repose upon it; it strengthens the soul and detaches us from ourselves; let us dwell upon it in peace as long as possible.

As to the manner of meditating, it should not be subtle, nor composed of long reasonings;

simple and natural reflections derived immediately from the subject of our thoughts are all that is required.

We need take a few truths; meditate upon these without hurry, without effort, and without seeking for far-fetched reflections.

Every truth should be considered with reference to its practical bearing. To receive it without employing all means to put it faithfully in practice at whatever cost, is to "suppress the truth in unrighteousness" (Rom. 1:18); it is a resistance to the truth impressed upon us, and of course, to the Holy Spirit. This is the most terrible of all unfaithfulness.

As to a method in prayer, each one must be guided by his own experience.

Those who find themselves profited in using a strict method need not depart from it, while those who cannot so confine themselves may make use of their own mode, without ceasing to respect that which has been useful to many, and which so many pious and experienced persons have highly recommended. A method is intended to assist; if it be found to embarrass instead of assist, the sooner it is discarded the better.

The most natural mode, at first, is to take a book, and to cease reading whenever we feel so inclined by the passage upon which we are engaged, and, whenever that no longer ministers to our interior nourishment, to begin again. As a general rule, those truths which we highly relish and which shed a degree of practical light upon the things which we are required to give up for God, are leadings of divine grace, which we should follow without hesitation. "The wind blows where it wishes" (John 3:8), and "Where the Spirit of the Lord is, there is liberty" (2 Cor. 3:17).

In the course of time the proportion of reflections and reasonings will diminish, and that of tender feelings, affecting views and desires, will increase as we become sufficiently instructed and convinced by the Holy Spirit. The heart is satisfied, nourished, warmed, set on fire; a word only will give it employment for a long time.

Finally, increase of prayer is indicated by an increase of simplicity and steadiness in our views, a great multitude of objects and considerations being no longer necessary. Our intercourse with God resembles that with a friend;

at first, there are a thousand things to be told and as many to be asked; but after a time, these diminish, while the pleasure of being together does not. Everything has been said, but the satisfaction of seeing each other, of feeling that one is near the other, or reposing in the enjoyment of a pure and sweet friendship, can be felt without conversation; the silence is eloquent and mutually understood. Each feels that the other is in perfect sympathy with him and that their two hearts are incessantly poured one into the other, and constitute but one.

Thus it is that in prayer, our communion with God becomes a simple and familiar union, far beyond the need of words. But let it be remembered that God Himself must alone institute this prayer within us; nothing would be more rash nor more dangerous than to dare to attempt it of ourselves.

We must suffer ourselves to be led step by step, by someone conversant with the ways of God, who may lay the immovable foundations of correct teaching, and of the complete death of self in everything.

Our leisure and our needs must regulate our retirements; *our needs*, because it is with the soul as with the body; when we can no longer work without nourishment, we must take it; we shall otherwise be in danger of fainting. *Our leisure*, because, this absolute necessity of food excepted, we must attend to duty before we seek enjoyment in spiritual exercises. The man who has public duties and spends the time appropriate to them in meditating in retirement, would miss of God while he was seeking to be united to Him.

True union with God is to do His will without ceasing, in spite of all our natural disinclination and in every duty of life, however disagreeable or mortifying.

As precautions against wanderings, we must avoid close and intimate intercourse with those who are not pious, especially when we have been before led astray by their infectious maxims. They will open our wounds afresh; they have a secret correspondence deep in our souls; there is there a soft and insinuating counselor who is always ready to blind and deceive us.

Would you judge of a man? Observe who are his companions. How can he who loves God, and who loves nothing except in and for God, enjoy the intimate companionship of those who neither love nor know God, and who look upon love to Him as a weakness? Can a heart full of God and sensible of its own frailty ever rest and be at ease with those who have no feelings in common with it, but who are ever seeking to rob it of its treasure? Their delights, and the pleasures of which Faith is the source, are incompatible.

I am well aware that we cannot, nay, that we ought not to break with those friends to whom we are bound by esteem of their natural amiability, by their services, by the tie of sincere friendship, or by the regard consequent upon mutual good offices. Friends whom we have treated with a certain familiarity and confidence would be wounded to the quick were we to separate from them entirely; we must gently and imperceptibly diminish our intercourse with them without abruptly declaring our alteration of sentiment; we may see them in private, distinguish them from our less intimate friends, and confide to them those matters in which their integrity and friendship enable them to give us good advice, and to think with us, although our reasons for so thinking are more pure and elevated than theirs. In short, we may continue to serve them, and to manifest all the attentions of a cordial friendship, without suffering our hearts to be embarrassed by them.

How perilous is our state without this precaution! If we do not, from the first, boldly adopt all measures to render our piety entirely free and independent of our unregenerate friends, it is threatened with a speedy downfall. If a man surrounded by such companions be of a yielding disposition and inflammable passions, it is certain that his friends, even the best-intentioned ones, will lead him astray.

They may be good, honest, faithful, and possessed of all those qualities which render friendship perfect in the eye of the world; but, for him, they are infected, and their amiability only increases the danger.

Those who have not this estimable character should be sacrificed at once; blessed are we, when a sacrifice that ought to cost us so little may avail to give us so precious a security for our eternal salvation!

Not only, then, should we be exceedingly careful whom we will see, but we must also reserve the necessary time that we may see God alone in prayer. Those who have stations of importance to fill have generally so many indispensable duties to perform that, without the greatest care in the management of their time, none will be left to be alone with God. If they have ever so little inclination for dissipation, the hours that belong to God and their neighbor disappear altogether.

We must be firm in observing our rules. This strictness seems excessive, but without it everything falls into confusion; we become dissipated, relaxed, and lose strength; we insensibly separate from God, surrender ourselves to all our pleasures, and only then begin to perceive that we have wandered, when it is almost hopeless to think of endeavoring to return.

Prayer, prayer! This is our only safety. "Blessed be God, who has not turned away my prayer, nor His mercy from me!" (Ps. 66:20). And to be faithful in prayer, it is indispensable that we should dispose all the employments of the day, with a regularity nothing can disturb.

God of love, how I cherish those times when I scamper to You like a child climbing onto her father's lap, eager for a chat and ready to pour out my problems to a sympathetic ear. But I confess those times aren't frequent or even the norm. Otherwise I would find it easier to wake up that hour earlier to spend time with You before the world rushes in. I would talk to You incessantly throughout the day, like people who spend their hours texting on a phone, only without the need of electronic devices. I pray that You will become ever more dear to me, firm in the foundation of Your agape love. Amen.

Sovereign God, You know what I need and which way I should go. You fashioned my days before I left my mother's womb. So why do I resist accepting Your best for me, when You say no to my prayers? You've put a lot of thought into the path I will take. Your righteousness makes it straight, and leads me beside still waters. When I am overwhelmed, You bring me to the Rock that is Higher than I. When enemies beset me, with David I pray that You will make my way smooth before me. I praise You when Your best for me brings glory to Your name and transforms me into the image of Your Son. I confess that I do not always ask according to Your purposes in my life. Forgive my doubt. Teach me to trust Your heart when I can't see Your hand at work. Amen.

Blessed God, You promise blessing for the woman who meditates on Your Word day and night. Oh, Lord, I desire for Your words to permeate my being. As I go about my daily life, bring the warning, promise, or instruction to mind when I need it most. Through Your Word, You prepare me to give an answer about You to my children, my friends, my coworkers. Teach me the discipline of connecting with You. Open my eyes to the time slot I can count on being left uninterrupted, and let me spend it with You. Bring people into my life to whom I may be accountable, that we may pray both for and with each other and encourage one another to fill our minds with truth. Forgive me when I neglect that spiritual discipline. Give me a hunger for what only You can provide. Amen.

My God and King, forgive me when I ignore the invitation to come into Your presence, when instead I value the companionship and comfort of flesh-and-blood. Sometimes I use things, too, entertainment in its multitude of forms. I confess I don't always know how to turn away people and their constant demands. But it's more than that. Reveal to me if I should sever ties with someone who has led me into sin. I confess the very thought makes me shiver. It feels self-righteous—but if I don't initiate some of that self-pruning, You may do it for me. Give me clarity instead of confusion, discipline instead of chaos. Thank You, Lord. Amen.

CHAPTER 5:
Disciples Taught to Pray, Part 1
Matthew Henry

One of His disciples said to Him,
"Lord, teach us to pray."
Luke 11:1

Prayer is one of the great laws of natural religion. That man is a brute, is a monster, that never prays, that never gives glory to his Maker, nor feels His favor, nor owns his dependence upon Him. One great design therefore of Christianity is to assist us in prayer, to enforce the duty upon us, to instruct us in it, and to encourage us to expect advantage by it.

In the book of Luke, we find Christ Himself "praying in a certain place," probably where He used to pray (11:1). As God, He was *prayed to;* as man, He *prayed;* and, though He was a Son, yet learned He this obedience. This evangelist has taken particular notice of Christ's praying often, more than any other of the evangelists: When He was baptized, He was praying (3:21); He "withdrew into the wilderness and prayed" (5:16); He "went out to the mountain to pray, and continued all night in prayer" (6:12); He was "alone praying" (9:18); soon after, He "went up on the mountain to pray," and as He prayed He was transfigured (9:28, 29). Thus, like a genuine son of David, He gave himself unto prayer (Ps. 109:4). Whether Christ was now *alone* praying, and the disciples only knew that He was so, or whether He prayed *with them*, is uncertain; it is most probable that they were joining with Him.

His disciples applied themselves to Him for direction in prayer. When He was praying, they asked, "Lord, teach us to pray." Note that the gifts and graces of others should excite us to covet earnestly the same. Their zeal should provoke us to a holy imitation and emulation; why should not we do as well as they? Observe: They came to Him with this request when He ceased; for they would not disturb Him when He was at prayer, no, not with this good motion. Everything is beautiful in its season. One of His disciples, in the name of the rest, and perhaps by their appointment, said, *Lord, teach us.* Though Christ is apt to teach, yet He will for this be inquired of, and His disciples must attend Him for instruction.

Their request in Luke 11:1 is, "Lord, teach us to pray"; or, give us a rule or model by which to go in praying, and put words into our mouths. It becomes the disciples of Christ to apply themselves to Him for instruction in prayer. *Lord, teach us to pray,* is itself a good prayer, and a very needful one, for it is a hard thing to pray well, and it is Jesus Christ only that can teach us, by His Word and Spirit, how to pray. Lord, teach me what it is to pray; Lord, excite and quicken me to the duty; Lord, direct me what to pray for; Lord, give me praying graces, that I may serve God acceptably in prayer; Lord, teach me to pray in proper words; give me a mouth and wisdom in prayer, that I may speak as I ought; *teach me what I shall say.*

Their plea is that He teach them "as John also taught his disciples." John took care to instruct his disciples in this necessary duty, and we would be taught as they were, for we have a better Master than they had. Dr. Lightfoot's notion of this is that, whereas the Jews' prayers were generally adorations, doxologies, and praises of God, John taught his disciples such prayers as were more filled up with petitions and requests; for it is said of them that they did *deeseis poiountai*—"make prayers" (Luke 5:33). The word signifies such prayers as are properly petitionary. "Now, Lord," the disciples asked, "teach us this, to be added to those benedictions of the name of God which we have been accustomed to from our childhood." According to this sense, Christ did there teach them a prayer consisting wholly of petitions, and even omitting the doxology which had been affixed; and the *Amen*, which was usually said in the giving of thanks (1 Cor. 14:16) and in the Psalms, is added to doxologies only. This disciple needed not to have urged John the Baptist's example: Christ was more ready to teach than ever John the Baptist was, and particularly taught to pray better than John did, or could, teach his disciples.

Christ gave them direction, much the same as He had given them before in His sermon upon the mount (Matt. 6:9–13).

We cannot think that they had forgotten

it, but they ought to have had further and fuller instructions, and He did not, as yet, think fit to give them any; when the Spirit should be poured out upon them from on high, they would find all their requests couched in these few words, and would be able, in words of their own, to expatiate and enlarge upon them. In Matthew, He had directed them to pray "in this manner." Luke's version (11:2) words the instruction thus: "When you pray, say"; which intimates that the Lord's prayer was intended to be used both as a *form* of prayer and a *directory*.

There are some differences between the Lord's prayer in Matthew and Luke, by which it appears that it was not the design of Christ that we should be *tied up* to these very words, for then there would have been no variation. Here is one difference in the translation only, which ought not to have been, when there is none in the original, and that is in the third petition: "As in heaven, so in earth" (KJV); whereas the words are the very same, and in the same order, as in Matthew. But there is a difference in the fourth petition. In Matthew we read, "Give us *this day* our daily bread," but in Luke we read, "Give us *day by day* our daily bread" (KJV)—*kath hemeran*. *Day by day*; that is, "Give us *each day* the bread which our bodies require, as they call for it," not, "Give us *this day* bread for many days to come," but as the Israelites had manna. He taught them to ask, "Let us have bread *today* for today, and *tomorrow* for tomorrow"; for thus we may be kept in a continual dependence upon God, as children upon their parents, and may have our mercies fresh from His hand daily, and may find ourselves under fresh obligations to do the work of every day in the day, according as the duty of the day requires, because we have from God the supplies of every day in the day, according as the necessity of the day requires.

There is, likewise, some difference in the fifth petition. In Matthew it is, "Forgive us our debts," as we forgive: In Luke, it is, "Forgive us our sins"; which proves that our sins are our debts. *For we forgive*; not that our forgiving those that have offended us can *merit* pardon from God, or be an inducement to Him to forgive us (He forgives for His own name's sake, and His Son's sake); but this is a very necessary qualification for forgiveness, and, if God has wrought it in us, we may plead that work of His grace for the enforcing of our petitions for the pardon of our sins: "Lord, forgive us, for Thou hast Thyself inclined us to forgive others." There is another addition here; we plead not only in general, We forgive "our debtors," but in particular, We profess to forgive "everyone who is indebted to us," without exception.

We so forgive our debtors as not to bear malice or ill will to any, but true love to all, without any exception whatsoever. Luke also omits the doxology and the Amen in the closing; for Christ would leave them at liberty to use that or any other doxology fetched out of David's psalms; or, rather, he left a vacuum here, to be filled up by a doxology more peculiar to the Christian institutes, ascribing glory to Father, Son, and Holy Ghost.

Yet it is, for substance, the same; and we shall therefore here only gather up some general lessons from it:

In prayer we ought to come to God as children to a Father, a common Father to us and all mankind but, in a peculiar manner, a Father to all the disciples of Jesus Christ. Let us, therefore, in our requests both for others and for ourselves, come to Him with a humble boldness, confiding in His power and goodness.

At the same time, and in the same petitions in which we address to God for ourselves, we should take in with us all the children of men, as God's creatures and our fellow creatures. A rooted principle of catholic charity and of Christian sanctified humanity should go along with us and dictate to us throughout this prayer, which is so worded as to be accommodated to that noble principle.

In order to confirm the habit of heavenly-mindedness in us, which ought to actuate and govern us in the whole course of our conversation, we should, in all our devotions, with an eye of faith, look heavenward and view the God we pray to as our Father in heaven, that we may make the upper world more familiar to us and may ourselves become better prepared for the future state.

In prayer, as well as in the tenor of our lives, we must "seek first the kingdom of God and His righteousness" (Matt. 6:33), by ascribing honor to His name, His *holy* name, and power to His government, both that of His providence in the world and that of His grace in the church. Oh, that both the one and the other may be more manifested, and we and others more manifestly brought into subjection to both!

The principles and practices of the upper world, the unseen world (which, therefore, by faith only we are apprized), are the great original—the *archetypon*, to which we should desire that the principles and practices of this lower world, both in others and in ourselves, may be more conformable. Those words, "on earth as it is in heaven," refer to all the first three petitions: "Father, let Your name be sanctified and glorified, and Your kingdom prevail, and Your will be done on this earth that is now alienated from Your service, as it is in yonder heaven that is entirely devoted to Your service."

Those who faithfully and sincerely mind the kingdom of God, and the righteousness thereof, may humbly hope that all other things, as far as to Infinite Wisdom seems good, shall be added to them, and they may, in faith, pray for them.

If our chief desire and care be that God's name may be sanctified, His kingdom come, and His will be done, we may then come boldly to the throne of grace for our daily bread, which will then be sanctified to us when we are sanctified to God, and God is sanctified by us.

In our prayers for temporal blessings, we must moderate our desires and confine them to a competency. The expression here used of "day by day" is the very same with "our daily bread"; and therefore some think that we must look for another signification of the word *epiousios* than that of "daily," which we give it, and that it means our "necessary bread," that bread that is suited to the craving of our nature, the fruit that is brought out of the earth for our bodies that are made of the earth and are earthly (Ps. 104:14).

Sins are debts which we are daily contracting, and which, therefore, we should every day pray for the forgiveness of.

We are not only going behind with our rent every day by *omissions* of duty and in duty, but are daily incurring the penalty of the law, as well as the forfeiture of our bond, by our *commissions.* Every day adds to the score of our guilt, and it is a miracle of mercy that we have so much encouragement given us to come every day to the throne of grace, to pray for the pardon of our sins of daily infirmity. God multiplies to pardon beyond seventy times seven.

We have no reason to expect, nor can we with any confidence pray, that God would forgive our sins against Him if we do not sincerely, and from a truly Christian principle of charity, forgive those who have at any time affronted us or been injurious to us. Though the words of our mouth be even this prayer to God, if the meditation of our heart at the same time be, as often it is, malice and revenge to our brethren, we are not accepted, nor can we expect an answer of peace.

Temptations to sin should be as much dreaded and deprecated by us as ruin by sin; and it should be as much our care and prayer to get the power of sin broken in us as to get the guilt of sin removed from us; and though temptation may be a charming, fawning, flattering thing, we must be as earnest with God that we may not be led into it as that we may not be led by that to sin, and by sin to ruin.

Finally, God is to be depended upon and sought unto for our deliverance from all evil;

and we should pray, not only that we may not be left to ourselves to run into evil, but that we may not be left to Satan to bring evil upon us. Dr. Lightfoot understands it of being delivered from the evil one, that is, the devil, and suggests that we should pray particularly against the apparitions of the devil and his possessions.

The disciples were employed to cast out devils, and therefore were concerned to pray that they might be guarded against the particular spite he would always be sure to have against them.

Dear Jesus, no wonder the disciples said, "Lord, teach us to pray." You not only taught with authority—Your prayers were different too. Your prayer habits both inspire and intimidate me. You got up in the middle of the night to spend long hours talking with Your Father. I confess I'm like the disciples, who, on the night You were betrayed, couldn't stay awake for an hour at the time of Your greatest need. Sometimes I even have a hard time spending five minutes in prayer. Like them, I long to pray as You did at Lazarus's grave. Father, I thank You that You have heard me. And I know that You always hear me (John 11:41–42). Thank you that my prayers continue an ongoing conversation. Lord, teach me to pray today and every day until You call me home. Amen.

Our heavenly Father, I join in prayer with those arising from homes across the world this day. May we bless Your holy name in word, thought, and deed. Use us to invite new citizens into Your Kingdom. May Your will be done in and through us. Give us our daily bread. We ask only for what

*we need, not what we want, and only enough
for today. If we have more than we need, instill
in us a desire to share. Point out any contempt or
bitterness in our hearts. Teach us to forgive
as we have been forgiven. Give us the
discernment to recognize the source of temptation
and deliver us from the same. And when
trials come, for they will, we ask for that
same deliverance. For Yours is the Kingdom
and the power and the glory forever. Amen.*

*Eternal God, You have given us the gift of time.
And we can pray both for temporal and for
eternal things. Teach me to discern between the
two. When I pray that Your name be made holy,
free my imagination to ask for the impossible in,
through, and around me and around the world.
Multiply my prayers for the here-and-now
to infinity. Provide food for my family—and the
millions of starving children around the world.
Heal my friend—and the thousands that lie
sick and dying. I ask for today's manna,
for strength and provision to get through
the next twenty-four hours. In Jesus'
name and for Your glory, amen.*

Author of forgiveness, You have forgiven me so much. Why do I struggle so to forgive others? Although I was responsible for the division between You and me, You initiated reconciliation. You not only took the first step, You took all the steps, to the point of giving Your Son to die in my place. Forgive me when I treat that sacrifice lightly. Scour my mind and heart when I refuse to forgive those who have hurt me. You cast my sin into the deepest sea and refuse to bring it up again. I remember harms done to me. Forgive me, change me, give me a heart of love! Oh, Lord, scrub bitterness from my heart that I may love You more freely and follow You more nearly. Show me what it means to love my neighbor—even those who hurt me—as I love myself. Amen.

CHAPTER 6:
Disciples Taught to Pray, Part 2
Matthew Henry

"Ask, and it will be given to you; seek, and you will find; knock, and it will be opened to you."
Luke 11:9

Jesus stirs up and encourages persistence, fervency, and constancy in prayer by showing that importunity will go far in our dealings with men. Consider the story He tells in Luke 11:5–8. Suppose a man, upon a sudden emergency, goes to borrow a loaf or two of bread of a neighbor at an unseasonable time of night, not for himself, but for his friend who came unexpectedly to him. His neighbor will be loath to accommodate him, for he has wakened him with his knocking and put him out of humor, and he has a great deal to say in his excuse. The door is shut and locked; his children are asleep in bed in the same room with him, and if he make a noise, he shall disturb them. His servants are asleep, and he cannot make them hear; and, for his own part, he shall catch cold if he rises to give the neighbor the bread. But his neighbor will have no nay, and therefore he continues knocking still and tells him he will do so till he has what he comes for; so that he must give it to him, to be rid of him. Thus, "because of his persistence he will rise and give him as many as he needs." Jesus speaks this parable with the same intent that He speaks of in Luke 18:1: "That men always ought to pray and not lose heart." Not that God can be wrought upon by persistence; we cannot be troublesome to Him, nor by being so change His counsels. We prevail with men by persistence because they are *displeased* with it, but with God because He is *pleased* with it.

Now this similitude may be of use to us to direct us in prayer. We must come to God with boldness and confidence for what we need, as a man does to the house of his neighbor or friend, who, he knows, loves him, and is inclined to be kind to him. We must come for bread, for that which is needful and which we cannot be without. We must come to Him by prayer for others as well as for ourselves.

This man did not come for bread for himself, but for his friend. The Lord accepted Job when he prayed for his friends (Job 42:10). We cannot come to God upon a more pleasing errand than when we come to Him for grace to enable us to do good, to feed many with our lips, and to entertain and edify those that come to us. We may also come with more boldness to God in a strait, if it be a strait that we have not brought ourselves into by our own folly and carelessness, but Providence has led us into it. This man would not have wanted bread if his friend had not come in unexpectedly. The care which Providence casts upon us, we may with cheerfulness cast back upon Providence. Thus, we ought to continue instant in prayer, and watch in the same with all perseverance.

Knowing that God enjoys our persistence should encourage us in prayer.

If persistence could prevail thus with a man who was angry at it, how much more will it do with a God who is infinitely more kind and ready to do good to us than we are to one another and who is not angry at our persistence, but accepts it, especially when it is looking for spiritual mercies. If He does not answer our prayers presently, yet He will in due time if we continue to pray.

Remember that God has promised to give us what we ask of Him. We have not only the goodness of nature to take comfort from, but the word which He has spoken as well: "Ask, and it will be given to you" (Luke 11:9); either the thing itself for which you ask or that which is equivalent; either the thorn in the flesh removed or grace sufficient for it. We have it from Christ's own mouth, who knows His Father's mind and in whom all promises are yea and amen. We must not only *ask,* but we must *seek.* In the use of means, we must second our prayers with our endeavors, and, in asking and seeking, we must continue *pressing,* still knocking at the same door, and we shall at length prevail, not only by our prayers in concert, but by our particular prayers: "Everyone who asks receives" (Matt. 7:8), even the humblest saint that asks in faith. "This poor man cried out, and the LORD heard him" (Ps. 34:6). When we ask of God those things which Christ has here directed us to ask, that His name may be sanctified, that His kingdom may come, and His will be done, in these requests we must be persistent, must never hold our peace day or night; we must not keep silence, nor give God any "rest till He establishes and till He makes Jerusalem a praise in the earth" (Isa. 62:6–7).

Christ gives us both instruction and encouragement in prayer from the consideration of our relation to God as a Father. Let any of you that is a father and knows the heart of a father, a father's affection to a child and care for a child, tell me, "If a son asks for bread from any father among you, will he give him a stone? Or if he asks for a fish, will he give him a serpent instead of a fish? Or if he asks for an egg, will he offer him a scorpion?" (Luke 11:11–12). You know you could not be so unnatural to your own children.

Christ goes on to apply this to the blessings of our *heavenly Father* in verse 13: "If you then, being evil, know how to give good gifts to your children, how much more will your heavenly Father give the Holy Spirit to those who ask Him!" He shall give *good things*; so it is in Matthew, as well.

Note that He directs us in *what to pray for.* We must ask for the Holy Spirit, not only as necessary in order to our praying well, but as inclusive of all the good things we are to pray for; we need no more to make us happy, for the Spirit is the worker of spiritual life, and the earnest of eternal life. The gift of the Holy Ghost is a gift we are every one of us concerned earnestly and constantly to pray for.

He *encourages* us in prayer by reminding us: "Your heavenly Father will give." It is in His power to give the Spirit; He has all good things to bestow, wrapped up in that one; but that is not all—it is in His promise, the gift of the Holy Ghost is in the covenant (Acts 2:33, 38), and it is here inferred from parents' readiness to supply their children's needs and gratify their desires when they are natural and proper. If the child ask for a serpent or a scorpion, the father, in kindness, will deny him, but not if he ask for what is needful and will be nourishing. When God's children ask for the Spirit, they do, in effect, ask for bread; for the Spirit is the staff of life; nay, He is the Author of the soul's life. If our earthly parents, though evil, be yet so kind, if they, though weak, be yet so knowing, that they not only give, but give with discretion, give what is best, in the best manner and time, much more will our heavenly Father, who infinitely excels the fathers of our flesh both in wisdom and goodness, give us His Holy Spirit. If earthly parents be willing to lay out for the education of their children, to whom they design to leave their estates, much more will our heavenly Father give the spirit of sons to all those whom He has predestinated to the inheritance of sons.

*Abba Father, You want to answer my prayers,
but You also desire me to pray persistently.
I confess I don't understand why You have
instructed me to continue asking, seeking, and
knocking. Perhaps it's like learning how to play
the piano. If everyone applauded the first time
I played a piece of music, why would I continue
to practice? I will only learn how to pray by
praying. Forgive me when I stop before I see
the answer—for people and nations in need of
Your saving grace, for relationships that need
to be reconciled, for habits and sins I struggle
with. Sometimes I accept the status quo and
cease asking. Today's needs crowd out yesterday's
requests. Make me far-sighted, that I may offer
up to You that unmet need, that future goal,
until You swing heaven's door open to an answer
beyond what I have dreamed. Amen.*

*Father God, how I thank You that I can lay my
needs before You, confident that You will supply all
my needs according to Your riches in glory. Bring to
mind the needs of those around me. Famine, both
physical and spiritual, starts in my neighborhood*

and spreads to the ends of the earth. I pray that those who don't know You will taste the Bread of Life, as You are called, and consume the good news with gladness of heart. Use me as part of the answer. If I have two coats, let me share one with someone who has none. Give me the heart and the words to speak of what I have seen and heard, to give You honor and gratitude. Amen.

Lord God, how I praise You that when this poor woman cried out, You heard me, and saved me out of all my troubles (Psalm 34:6), even when I didn't recognize it as deliverance. Because You delivered me in the past, I come in confidence that You will do the same today. I thank You for the faith experience. Open my eyes to recognize the answered prayers that didn't match my expectations. When I prayed for money to make car payments and You taught me the grace of riding the bus. When I prayed for my children to respond to my discipline and You sent someone else to intervene. I thank You for the lessons today's problems teach me. Once Your gifts I wanted, now the Giver own—Yourself, alone, apart from any gifts You may give. Amen.

Heavenly Father, You gave us a model prayer that rolls off my lips as if I am reciting a favorite

poem, the rhythm, the cadence, making music to
my ears. Our Father in heaven, hallowed be Your
name. Your Kingdom come, Your will be done, on
earth as it is in heaven. There is such impact and
power in those simple words. But I dare to use
my own humble words. May all that we do as
individuals, and as congregations and cities and
nations, further Your Kingdom. When faced with
an unclear decision, show us which choice will
glorify and honor You as holy and draw Your
Kingdom closer. How much simpler my choices
would be if I kept those standards in mind.
Show me when I go astray, and forgive me
for choosing less than Your best.
In Jesus' name, amen.

CHAPTER 7:
Prayer Must Be Specific
ANDREW MURRAY

So Jesus answered and said to him,
"What do you want Me to do for you?"
MARK 10:51

The blind man had been crying out loudly, and that a great deal, "Son of David, have mercy on me!" (Mark 10:47). The cry had reached the ear of the Lord, and He knew what the man wanted and was ready to grant it to him. But before He does it, He asks him, *"What do you want* Me to do for you?" He wants to hear from the man's own lips, not only the general request for mercy, but the distinct expression of what his desire was. Until he speaks it out, he is not healed.

There is now still many a petitioner to whom the Lord puts the same question, and who cannot, until it is answered, get the aid he asks. Our prayers must not be a vague appeal to His mercy or an indefinite cry for blessing, but a distinct expression of definite need. Not that His loving heart does not understand our cries or is not ready to hear. But He desires it for our own sakes. Such definite prayer teaches us to know our own needs better. It demands time, thought, and self-examination to find out what our greatest need really is.

It searches us and puts us to the test as to whether our desires are honest and real, such as we are ready to persevere in.

It leads us to judge whether our desires are according to God's Word, and whether we really believe we shall receive the things we ask for. It helps us to wait for the specific answer and to recognize it when it comes.

And yet how much of our prayer is vague and pointless. Some cry for mercy, but don't take the trouble to know what mercy must do for them. Others ask, perhaps, to be delivered from sin, but do not begin by bringing any sin by name from which the deliverance can be claimed. Still others pray for God's blessing on those around them, for the outpouring of God's Spirit on their land or on the world, and yet they have no special field where they wait and expect to see the answer. To every one of these the Lord says, "What do you want Me to do for you?"

Every Christian has only limited powers, and just as he must have his own specific field of labor in which he works, so it is with his prayers, too. Each believer has his own circle: family, friends, and neighbors. If he were to take one or more of these by name, he would find this really brings him into the training school of faith, which leads to personal and pointed dealing with his God. It is when in such distinct matters we have in faith claimed and received answers that our more general prayers will be believing and effective.

We all know with what surprise the whole civilized world heard of the way in which trained troops were repulsed by the Transvaal Boers at Majuba. And to what did they owe their success? In the armies of Europe, the solider fires on the enemy standing in large masses, and never thinks of seeking an aim for every bullet.

In hunting game, the Boer had learned a different lesson: his practiced eye knew to send every bullet on its special mission, to seek and find its man. Such aiming must gain the day in the spiritual world, too.

As long as in prayer we just pour out our hearts in a multitude of petitions without taking time to see whether every petition is sent with the purpose and expectation of getting an answer, not many will reach the mark. But if, as in silence of the soul we bow before the Lord, we were ready to answer questions such as these: What is now really my desire? Do I desire it in faith, expecting to receive? Am I now ready to place and leave it there in the Father's bosom? Is it settled between God and me that I am to have the answer?—we should learn to pray in such a way that God will see and we would know what we really expect.

It is for this reason, among others, that the Lord warns us against the vain repetitions of the Gentiles, who expect to be heard because they pray so much (see Matt. 6:7–8). We often hear prayers of great earnestness and fervor, in which a multitude of petitions are poured forth, but to which the Savior would undoubtedly answer, "What do you want Me to do for you?"

If I am in a strange land, in the interests of the business my father owns, I would certainly write two different sorts of letters home. There will be family letters giving expression to the interaction to which affection prompts, and there will be business letters containing orders for what I need. There may also be letters in which both are found. The answers will correspond to the letters. To each sentence of the letters containing the family news, I do not expect a special answer. But for each order I send, I am confident of an answer as to whether the desired article has been sent. In our dealings with God, the business element must not be lacking.

With our expressions of need and sin, of love and faith and consecration, there must be the specific statement of what we ask and expect to receive. It is in the answer that the Father loves to give us a proof of His approval and acceptance.

But the word of the Master teaches us more. He does not say, "What do you *wish*?" but "What do you *want*?" One often wishes for a thing without willing it.

I wish to have a certain item, but I find the price is too high, so I decide not to take it. I *wish* but do not *will* to have it. The lazy man wishes to be rich, but does not will it. Many a man wishes to be saved, but perishes because he does not will it. The will rules the whole heart and life. If I really will to have something that is within my reach, I do not rest until I have it. When Jesus asks us, "What do you want?" He asks whether it is indeed our purpose to have what we ask for at any price, however great the sacrifice. Do you really will to have it enough that, though He waits to answer, you will not hold your peace until He hears you? Sadly, many prayers are wishes sent up for a short time and then forgotten, or sent up year after year as a matter of duty, while we remain content with the prayer without the answer.

But, it may be asked, is it not best to make our wishes known to God and then leave it to Him to decide what is best, without our seeking to assert our will? By no means! This is the very essence of the prayer of faith to which Jesus sought to train His disciples, that it does not only make known its desire and then leave the decision to God. That would be the prayer of submission for cases in which we cannot know God's will. But the prayer of faith, finding God's will in some promise of the Word, pleads for that until it comes.

In Matthew 9:28, we read that Jesus said to the blind man, "*Do you believe* that I am able to do this?" In Mark He said, "*What do you want* Me to do for you?*" (10:51). In both cases, He said that faith had saved them. And He said to the Syrophoenician woman, too, "Great is your faith! Let it be to you as you desire" (Matt. 15:28). Faith is nothing but the purpose of the will resting on God's Word and saying, "I must have it." To believe truly is to will firmly.

But is not such a will at odds with our dependence on God and our submission to Him? By no means! Rather, it is the true submission that honors God. It is only when the child has yielded his own will in entire surrender to the Father that he receives from the Father the liberty and power to will what he desires. But when once the believer has accepted the will of God, as revealed through the Word and the Spirit, as his will, too, then it is the will of God that His child should use this renewed will in His service. The will is the highest power of the soul. Grace wants above everything to sanctify and restore this will, one of the chief traits of God's image, to full and free exercise. As a son who lives only for his father's interests, who seeks not his own but his father's will, is trusted by the father with his business, so God speaks to His child in all truth, "What do you want?"

It is often spiritual complacency that, under the appearance of humility, professes to have no will because it fears the trouble of searching for the will of God, or, when that will is found, the struggle of claiming it in faith. True humility is always accompanied by strong faith, which only seeks to know what is according to the will of God and then boldly claims the fulfillment of the promise: "You will ask what you desire, and it shall be done for you" (John 15:7).

"LORD, TEACH US TO PRAY."

Lord Jesus! Teach me to pray with all my heart and strength so that there may be no doubt with You or with me about what I have asked. May I know so well what I desire that, even as my requests are recorded in heaven, I can also record them on earth and note each answer as it comes. And may my faith in what Your Word has promised be so clear that the Spirit may indeed work within me the liberty to will that it will come. Lord! Renew, strengthen, and sanctify wholly my will for the work of effectual prayer.

Blessed Savior! I pray that You will reveal to me the wonderful grace You show us, thus asking us to say what we desire that You should do, and promising to do whatever we desire. Son of God! I cannot fully understand it. I can only believe that You have, indeed, redeemed us wholly for Yourself, and that You seek to make the will, as our noblest part, Your most effective servant. Lord! I most unreservedly yield my will to You as the power through which Your Spirit is to rule my whole being. Let Him take possession of it, lead it into the truth of Your promises, and make it so strong in prayer that I may always hear Your voice saying, "Great is your faith! Let it be to you as you desire." Amen.

Omniscient God, You know when a bird loses a feather and the number of hairs caught in my hairbrush. You expect the same kind of attention to detail from me. Right now, I face a decision about whether or not to move. You've heard my whining and my indecision. Daily You supply me with the details I need to make my choice, yet still I dally. Now You want more from me. Move me from praying "Lord, help me!" to action. Open my eyes of faith to the mile markers on the road ahead. Thank You for Your answer. Amen.

Omnipresent God, I'm often tempted to take shortcuts to prayer, to summarize my requests like Tiny Tim and say, "God bless us, every one." Other times, I'm like a child saying her bedtime prayers, mentioning people by name but little more. How can I expect to recognize Your answers to such general prayers? Bring to mind the principles and promises of Your Word to ask for those I pray for. That my son will walk in integrity, keep his promises, and fulfill his commitments. That my pastor will love You with all his heart, mind, soul, and strength. That our

nation's leaders will submit to Your authority.
Forgive me when I fail to pray when
I have promised. Great Teacher, make me an
eager pupil in the school of prayer. Amen.

Wonderful Counselor, You know what is in my
heart. You sift my requests, sorting my wants
from my wishes. You plumb the depths of my
being, weighing my sincerity. When I ask to be
rescued from a bad situation, am I ready for You
to change me, and not my circumstances? When
You don't answer right away, do I give up and
move on to the next item on my prayer list? I
confess I have many prayer projects that I have
abandoned in search of the next tool to encourage
me to pray better. Forgive my inconsistency.
Make me hungry for the closeness of a continual
conversation with You, where the disciplines
of prayer become the highlight of my day,
and not a duty to be discharged as
quickly as possible. Amen.

My Shepherd, You lead me in Your paths for
Your name's sake. I confess I'm sometimes blind
to that path, as blind to Your will as a sightless
man at a crossroads without a map. You promise
to give wisdom when I ask, but I confess I often

ask amiss. I want tomorrow's answers today, step-by-step directions laid out for me like a computer program, so that I can anticipate every stopping point and every challenging stretch of road. Thank You for enough light for today. Why do I ask for Your plans for my summer when it's still winter? Let me spend the winter and spring seasons in Your Word, so that I will understand Your will when summer is upon me. Amen.

CHAPTER 8:
The Faith That Takes
ANDREW MURRAY

*"Therefore I say to you, whatever things you ask
when you pray, believe that you receive them,
and you will have them."*
MARK 11:24

What a promise! So large, so divine that
our little hearts cannot take it in, and
in every possible way we seek to limit it to what
we think is safe or probable, instead of allowing it, in its quickening power and energy, just
as He gave it, to enter in and to enlarge our
hearts to the measure of what His love and
power are really ready to do for us.

Faith is very far from being a mere conviction of the truth of God's Word or a con-
clusion drawn from certain premises. It is the
ear that has heard God say what He will do,
the eye that has seen Him doing it. Therefore,
where there is true faith, it is impossible for

the answer not to come. If we only see to it that we do the one thing that He asks of us as we pray: "Believe that you receive," He will see to it that He does the thing He has promised: "You will have them."

The keynote of Solomon's prayer (2 Chron. 6:4), "Blessed be the LORD God of Israel, who has fulfilled with His hands what He spoke with His mouth," is the keynote of all true prayer. It is the joyful adoration of a God whose *hand* always secures the fulfillment of what His *mouth* has spoken. Let us in this spirit listen to the promise Jesus gives, for each part of it has a divine message.

Whatever things. At this first word our human wisdom begins to doubt and ask, "Can this possibly be literally true?" But if it isn't, why did the Master speak it, using the very strongest expression He could find: "whatever things." And it is not as if this were the only time He spoke that way. Is it not He who also said, "If you can believe, all things are possible to him who believes" (Mark 9:23), and "If you have faith as a mustard seed. . .nothing will be impossible for you" (Matt. 17:20)? Faith is so wholly the work of God's Spirit through His word in the prepared heart of the believing disciple that it is impossible for the fulfillment not to come. Faith is the pledge and forerunner of the coming answer.

Yes, "whatever things you ask in prayer, believing, you will receive" (Matt. 21:22). The tendency of human reason is to interpose here with certain qualifying clauses, such as "if expedient" or "if according to God's will," to break the force of a statement that appears dangerous.

Let us beware of dealing this way with the Master's words. His promise is most literally true. He wants His often-repeated "whatever things" to enter into our hearts and reveal to us how mighty the power of faith is, how truly the Head calls the members to share with Him in His power, how wholly our Father places His power at the disposal of the child who wholly trusts Him. In this "whatever things," faith is to have its food and strength: As we weaken it, we weaken faith.

The "whatever" is unconditional. The only condition is what is implied in the believing. Before we can believe, we must find out and know what God's will is. Believing is the exercise of a soul surrendered and given up to the influence of the Word and the Spirit. But when we believe, nothing shall be impossible. God forbid that we should try to bring down His *all things* to the level of what we think is possible. Rather, let us now simply take Christ's "whatever" as the measure and the hope of our faith. It is a seed-word that will, if taken just as He gives it and kept in the heart, germinate and take root, fill our life with its fullness, and bring forth abundant fruit.

Ask in prayer. "Whatever things you ask when you pray." It is in prayer that these "whatever things" are to be brought to God, to be asked for and received from Him. The faith that receives them is the fruit of the prayer. In one aspect, there must be faith before there can be prayer, but in another, the faith is the result and the growth of prayer. In the personal presence of the Savior, and in communication with Him, faith rises to grasp what at first appeared too high. It is in prayer that we hold up our desire to the light of God's holy will, that our motives are tested, and that proof is given whether we ask, indeed, in the name of Jesus and only for the glory of God. It is in prayer that we wait for the leading of the Spirit to show us whether we are asking for the right thing and in the right spirit. It is in prayer that we become aware of our lack of faith, that we are led to say to the Father that we do believe, and that we prove the reality of our faith by the confidence with which we persevere. It is in prayer that Jesus teaches and inspires faith. He who waits to pray, or loses heart in prayer because he doesn't yet feel the faith needed to get the answer, will never learn to believe. He who begins to pray and ask will find the Spirit of faith is given nowhere so surely as at the foot of the Throne.

Believe that you receive. It is clear that what we are to believe is that we receive the very things we ask. The Savior does not hint that because the Father knows what is best, He may give us something else. The very mountain that faith tells to depart is cast into the sea.

There is a prayer in which, when in everything we make our requests known with prayer and supplication, the reward is the sweet peace of God in our hearts and minds (see Phil. 4:6–7). This is the prayer of trust. It has reference to things which we cannot find out if God is going to give them. As children, we make known our desires in countless things of daily life and then leave it to the Father to give or not as He thinks best. But the prayer of faith of which Jesus speaks is something higher, something different. When, whether in the greater interests of the Master's work or in the lesser concerns of our daily life, the soul is led to see how there is nothing that so honors the Father like the faith that is assured that He will do what He has said in giving us whatever we ask for—and takes its stand on the promise as brought home by the Spirit—it may know with certainty that it receives exactly what it asks. Observe how clearly the Lord states this in Mark 11:23: "Whoever. . .does not doubt in his heart, but believes that *those things he says* will be done, he will have whatever he says." This is the blessing of the prayer of faith of which Jesus speaks.

"Believe that *you receive*." This is the word of central importance, of which the meaning is too often misunderstood. Believe that you receive—now, while praying—the thing you ask for. It may only be later that you shall have it in personal experience; that you shall see what you believe. But now, without seeing, you are to believe that it has already been given to you by the Father in heaven. The receiving or accepting of an answer to prayer is just like receiving or accepting Jesus or of pardon: It is a spiritual thing, an act of faith separate from all feeling. When I come as a supplicant and ask for forgiveness, I believe Jesus in heaven is for me, and so I receive or take from Him. When I come as a supplicant for a specific gift that is according to God's Word, I must believe that what I ask is given to me. I believe that I have it, I hold it in faith, and I thank God that it is mine. "And if we know that He hears us, whatever we ask, we know that we have the petitions that we have asked of Him" (1 John 5:15).

And you will have them. That is, the gift that we first hold in faith as bestowed on us in heaven will also become ours in personal experience. But will it be necessary to pray longer once we know we have been heard and have received what we asked? There are cases in which such prayer will not be needed, in which the blessing is ready to break through at once, if we simply hold firmly our confidence and prove our faith by praising for what we have received, even in the face of our not yet having it in experience. There are other cases, however, in which the faith that has received needs to be still further tested and strengthened in persevering prayer. Only God knows when everything in and around us is fully ripe for the manifestation of the blessing that has been given to faith. Elijah knew for certain that rain would come, for God had promised it. And yet he had to pray the seven times. And that prayer was no show or play. It was an intense spiritual reality both in the heart of him who lay there pleading, and in heaven, where it has its effectual work to do. (See 1 Kings 18:41–46.)

It is "through *faith and patience* [we] inherit the promises" (Heb. 6:12). Faith says most confidently, "I have received it." Patience perseveres in prayer until the gift bestowed in heaven is seen on earth. "Believe that you receive them, and you will have." Between the *you receive* in heaven and the *will have* of earth is the keyword *believe*. Believing praise and prayer is the link.

And now, remember one more thing: It is Jesus who said this. As we see heaven opened to us and the Father on the throne offering to give us whatever we ask for in faith, our hearts feel full of shame that we have so little made use of our privilege, and full of fear that our weak faith still fails to grasp what is so clearly placed within our reach. There is one thing that must make us strong and full of hope: It is Jesus who brought us this message from the Father.

He Himself, when He was on earth, lived the life of faith and prayer. It was when the disciples expressed their surprise at what He had done to the fig tree that He told them that the very same life He led could be theirs, that they could not only command the fig tree but the very mountain, and it must obey. And He is our life. All He was on earth, He is in us now. All He teaches, He really gives. He is Himself the Author and the Perfecter of our faith. He gives the spirit of faith.

Let us not be afraid that such faith isn't meant for us. It is meant for every child of the Father and it is within reach of anyone who will be childlike, yielding himself to the

Father's will and love and trusting the Father's Word and power.

Dear fellow Christians! Let the thought that this Word comes through Jesus, God's Son and our Brother, give us courage. And let our answer be, "Yes, blessed Lord, we do believe Your Word. We do believe so that we may receive."

"LORD, TEACH US TO PRAY."

Blessed Lord! You came from the Father to show us all His love and all the treasures of blessing that love is waiting to bestow. Lord, You have this day again thrown the gates so wide open and given us such promises concerning our liberty in prayer that we must blush that our poor hearts have so little taken it in. It has been too large for us to believe.

Lord! We now look up to You to teach us to take and keep and use Your precious Word: "Whatever things you ask when you pray, believe that you receive them." Blessed Jesus! It is in You our faith must be rooted if it is to grow strong. Your work has freed us wholly from the power of sin and has opened the way to the Father. Your love always longs to bring us into the full fellowship of Your glory and power. Your Spirit is constantly drawing us upward into a life of perfect faith and confidence. We are assured that in Your teaching we will learn to pray the prayer of faith. You will train us to pray so that we believe that we receive, to believe that we really have what we ask for.

Lord! Teach me to know and trust and love You, to live and abide in You in such a way that all my prayers rise up and come before God in You, that my soul may have in You the assurance that I am heard. Amen.

*Giving God, no matter how far we progress,
You are always ahead of us, beyond us, planning
to delight us with good things beyond our
comprehension. My eye has not seen, my ear has
not heard, nor has it entered into my heart the
things You have prepared for those who love You
(1 Corinthians 2:9). I thank You for the gift of
faith to accept those unseen things as fact. Show
me how to exercise my faith muscles. When I pray
for my child to grow in faith, may I hear him
praising Your name. When I pray for my
enemies, fill my heart with love for them.
When the answer comes, I will lift my voice
in praise for fulfilling what I have
already seen with the eyes
of faith. Amen.*

*Lord God, forgive me for giving up when prayer
is a struggle, when I feel like a failure because my
mountains haven't budged. In those times, teach
me about faith, how to choose to believe in spite
of my feelings and doubts. Like the father of the
epileptic child in scripture, I cry, Lord, I believe;
help my unbelief (Mark 9:24)! When that is all*

*the faith I have, to recognize that You alone can
supply what I need. How I praise You for Your
delight in my faltering, stumbling steps of faith.
I have to crawl in prayer before I can learn
to run. Let me never fail to pray because
I feel like it's not working. You will
hear and answer. Amen.*

*Faithful God, sometimes I pray for something
that won't happen during my lifetime. That's
hard, Lord—to pray for something I may never
see come to pass this side of heaven. Or I want
an answer now and You ask me to repeat my
prayers. Israel needed rain the first time the
prophet Elijah prayed, but he had to repeat the
prayer seven times before the tiny cloud appeared
in the sky. Forgive me when I give up after
the third attempt and then blame You for not
answering. I'm like a child, wanting immediate
gratification. Grow me into a mature believer,
willing to accept delayed gratification. I thank
You for Your peace that guards my heart and
mind through Christ Jesus. In Jesus' name, amen.*

*Heavenly Father, how blessed I am to call You
Father. I'm an insider! You chose me! It's all
about You. You redeemed me, You predestined me,*

You gave me the Spirit of adoption—and made me Your heir. Wow! How can that be? I am such a lowly, unworthy creature. You long to shower me with my inheritance, but I tend to hold back, waiting in the wings, hesitating to claim what is rightfully mine. Open my eyes to the truth, that I may see myself transformed into Your likeness. May I approach Your throne of grace with the confidence of Your daughter and heir. You will not turn me away. Amen!

CHAPTER 9:
Hindrances to Prayer
R. A. TORREY

You ask and do not receive,
because you ask amiss.
JAMES 4:3

We have gone very carefully into the positive conditions of prevailing prayer; but there are some things which hinder prayer. These God has made very plain in His Word.

The first hindrance to prayer we will find in James 4:3: "You ask and do not receive, because you ask amiss, that you may spend it on your pleasures."

A selfish purpose in prayer robs prayer of power. Very many prayers are selfish.

These may be prayers for things for which it is perfectly proper to ask, for things which it is the will of God to give, but the motive of the prayer is entirely wrong, and so the prayer falls powerless to the ground. The true purpose in prayer is that God may be glorified in the answer.

If we ask any petition merely that we may receive something to use in our pleasures or in our own gratification in one way or another, we "ask amiss" and need not expect to receive what we ask.

This explains why many prayers remain unanswered.

For example, many a woman is praying for the conversion of her husband.

That certainly is a most proper thing to ask; but many a woman's motive in asking for the conversion of her husband is entirely improper; it is selfish. She desires that her husband may be converted because it would be so much more pleasant for her to have a husband who sympathized with her; or it is so painful to think that her husband might die and be lost forever. For some such selfish reason as this, she desires to have her husband converted. The prayer is purely selfish. Why should a woman desire the conversion of her husband? First of all and above all, that God may be glorified; because she cannot bear the thought that God the Father should be dishonored by her husband trampling underfoot the Son of God.

Many pray for a revival. That certainly is a prayer that is pleasing to God; it is along the line of His will; but many prayers for revivals are purely selfish. The churches desire revivals in order that the membership may be increased, in order that the church may have a position of more power and influence in the community, in order that the church treasury may be filled, in order that a good report may be made at the presbytery or conference or association.

For such low purposes as these churches and ministers oftentimes pray for a revival, and oftentimes, too, God does not answer the prayer. Why should we pray for a revival? For the glory of God, because we cannot endure it that God should continue to be dishonored by the worldliness of the church, by the sins of unbelievers, by the proud unbelief of the day; because God's Word is being made void; in order that God may be glorified by the outpouring of His Spirit on the Church of Christ. For these reasons first of all and above all, we should pray for a revival.

Many a prayer for the Holy Spirit is a purely selfish prayer. It certainly is God's will

to give the Holy Spirit to them that ask Him—
He has told us so plainly in His Word (Luke
11:13), but many a prayer for the Holy Spirit
is hindered by the selfishness of the motive
that lies behind the prayer. Men and women
pray for the Holy Spirit in order that they may
be happy, or in order that they may be saved
from the wretchedness of defeat in their lives,
or in order that they may have power as Christian workers, or for some other purely selfish
motive. Why should we pray for the Spirit? In
order that God may no longer be dishonored
by the low level of our Christian lives and by
our ineffectiveness in service; in order that God
may be glorified in the new beauty that comes
into our lives and the new power that comes
into our service.

The second hindrance to prayer we find
in Isaiah 59:1–2: "Behold, the LORD's hand is
not shortened, that it cannot save; nor His ear
heavy, that it cannot hear. But your iniquities
have separated you from your God; and your
sins have hidden His face from you, so that He
will not hear."

Sin hinders prayer. Many a man prays and
prays and prays, and gets absolutely no answer

to his prayer. Perhaps he is tempted to think that it is not the will of God to answer, or he may think that the days when God answered prayer, if He ever did, are over. So the Israelites seem to have thought. They thought that the Lord's hand was shortened, that it could not save, and that His ear had become heavy that it could no longer hear.

"Not so," said Isaiah. "God's ear is just as open to hear as ever, His hand just as mighty to save; but there is a hindrance.

"That hindrance is your own sins. Your iniquities have separated you and your God, and your sins have hid His face from you that He will not hear."

It is so today. Many a man is crying to God in vain, simply because of sin in his life. It may be some sin in the past that has been unconfessed and unjudged; it may be some sin in the present that is cherished, very likely is not even looked upon as sin, but there the sin is, hidden away somewhere in the heart or in the life, and God "will not hear" because of it.

Anyone who finds his prayers ineffective should not conclude that the thing which he asks of God is not according to His will, but should go alone with God with the psalmist's prayer, "Search me, O God, and know my heart; try me, and know my anxieties; and see if there is any wicked way in me" (Ps. 139:23–24), and wait before Him until He puts His finger upon the thing that is displeasing in His sight. Then this sin should be confessed and put away.

I well remember a time in my life when I was praying for two definite things that it seemed that I must have or God would be dishonored; but the answer did not come.

I awoke in the middle of the night in great physical suffering and great distress of soul. I cried to God for these things, reasoned with Him as to how necessary it was that I get them, and get them at once; but no answer came. I asked God to show me if there was anything wrong in my own life. Something came to my mind that had often come to it before, something definite but which I was unwilling to confess as sin. I said to God, "If this is wrong I will give it up," but still no answer came. In my innermost heart, though I had never admitted it, I knew it was wrong.

At last I said: "This is wrong. I have sinned.

I will give it up." I found peace. In a few moments I was sleeping like a child.

In the morning I woke well in body, and the money that was so much needed for the honor of God's name came.

Sin is an awful thing, and one of the most awful things about it is the way it hinders prayer, the way it severs the connection between us and the Source of all grace and power and blessing. Anyone who would have power in prayer must be merciless in dealing with his own sins. "If I regard iniquity in my heart, the Lord will not hear" (Ps. 66:18). So long as we hold on to sin or have any controversy with God, we cannot expect Him to heed our prayers.

If there is anything that constantly comes up in your moments of close communion with God, that is the thing that hinders prayer: Put it away.

The third hindrance to prayer is found in Ezekiel 14:3: "Son of man, these men have set up their idols in their hearts, and put before them that which causes them to stumble into iniquity. Should I let Myself be inquired of at all by them?"

Idols in the heart cause God to refuse to listen to our prayers! What is an idol? An idol is anything that takes the place of God, anything that is the supreme object of our affection. God alone has the right to the supreme place in our hearts. Everything and everyone else must be subordinate to Him.

Many a man makes an idol of his wife. Not that a man can love his wife any too much, but he can put her in the wrong place, he can put her before God—and when a man regards his wife's pleasure before God's pleasure, when he gives her the first place and God the second place, his wife is an idol, and God cannot hear his prayers.

Many a woman makes an idol of her children. Not that we can love our children too much. The more dearly we love Christ, the more dearly we love our children; but we can put our children in the wrong place, we can put them before God and their interests before God's interests. When we do this our children are our idols.

Many a man makes an idol of his reputation or his business. When reputation or business is put before God, God cannot hear the prayers of such a man.

One great question for us to decide, if we would have power in prayer, is *Is God absolutely first?* Is He before wife, before children, before reputation, before business, before our own lives? If not, prevailing prayer is impossible.

God often calls our attention to the fact that we have an idol by not answering our prayers. That leads us to inquire as to why our prayers are not answered, and so we discover the idol. When we put it away, God hears our prayers.

The fourth hindrance to prayer is found in Proverbs 21:13: "Whoever shuts his ears to the cry of the poor will also cry himself and not be heard."

There is perhaps no greater hindrance to prayer than stinginess, the lack of liberality toward the poor and toward God's work. It is the one who gives generously to others who receives generously from God.

"Give, and it will be given to you: good measure, pressed down, shaken together, and running over will be put into your bosom. For with the same measure that you use, it will be measured back to you" (Luke 6:38). The generous man is the mighty man of prayer. The stingy man is the powerless man of prayer.

One of the most wonderful statements about prevailing prayer is found in 1 John 3:22: "Whatever we ask we receive from Him, because we keep His commandments and do those things that are pleasing in His sight." This statement is made in direct connection with generosity toward the needy. In the context, we are told that it is when we love, not in word or in tongue but in deed and in truth; when we open our hearts toward the brother in need, it is then and only then that we have confidence toward God in prayer.

Many a man or woman who is seeking to find the secret of their powerlessness in prayer need not seek far; it is nothing more nor less than downright stinginess. George Muller was a mighty man of prayer because he was a mighty giver. What he received from God never stuck to his fingers; he immediately passed it on to others. He was constantly receiving because he was constantly giving. When one thinks of the selfishness of the professing church today, it is no wonder that the church has so little power in prayer. If we would get from God, we must give to others.

Perhaps the most wonderful promise in the Bible in regard to God's supplying our need is found in Philippians 4:19, "And my God shall supply all your need according to His riches in glory by Christ Jesus." This glorious promise was made to the Philippian church in immediate connection with their generosity.

The fifth hindrance to prayer is found in Mark 11:25: "And whenever you stand praying, if you have anything against anyone, forgive him, that your Father in heaven may also forgive you your trespasses."

An unforgiving spirit is one of the commonest hindrances to prayer. Prayer is answered on the basis that our sins are forgiven; God cannot deal with us on the basis of forgiveness while we are harboring ill will against those who have wronged us.

Anyone who is nursing a grudge against another has fast closed the ear of God against his own petition.

How many there are crying to God for the conversion of husband, children, friends— and wondering why it is that their prayers are not answered, when the whole secret is some grudge that they have in their hearts against someone who has injured them, or who they fancy has injured them. Many a mother and father are allowing their children to go down to eternity unsaved, for the miserable gratification of hating someone else.

The sixth hindrance to prayer is found in 1 Peter 3:7: "Husbands, likewise, dwell with [your wives] with understanding, giving honor to the wife, as to the weaker vessel, and as being heirs together of the grace of life, that your prayers may not be hindered."

Here we are plainly told that a wrong relation between husband and wife is a hindrance to prayer. In many a case, the prayers of husbands are hindered because of their failure of duty toward their wives.

On the other hand, it is also doubtless true that the prayers of wives are hindered because of their failure in duty toward their husbands. If husbands and wives should seek diligently to find the cause of their unanswered prayers, they would often find it in their relations to one another.

Many a man who makes great pretentions to piety and is very active in Christian work, shows but little consideration in his treatment of his wife, and is oftentimes unkind, if not brutal; then he wonders why it is that his prayers are not answered. The verse that we have just quoted explains the seeming mystery. On the other hand, many a woman who is very devoted to the church and very faithful in attendance upon all services, treats her husband with the most unpardonable neglect, is cross and peevish toward him, wounds him by the sharpness of her speech and by her ungovernable temper; then she wonders why it is that she has no power in prayer.

There are other things in the relations of husbands and wives which doubtless are oftentimes a hindrance in approaching God in prayer. There is much of sin covered up under the holy name of marriage that is a cause of spiritual deadness and of powerlessness in prayer. Any man or woman whose prayers seem to bring no answer should spread their whole married life out before God, and ask Him to put His finger upon anything in it that is displeasing in His sight.

The seventh hindrance to prayer is found in James 1:5–7: "If any of you lacks wisdom, let him ask of God, who gives to all liberally and without reproach, and it will be given to him. But let him ask in faith, with no doubting, for he who doubts is like a wave of the sea driven and tossed by the wind. For let not that man suppose that he will receive anything from the Lord."

Prayers are hindered by unbelief. God demands that we shall believe His Word absolutely. To question it is to make Him a liar. Many of us do that when we plead His promises, and is it any wonder that our prayers are not answered? How many prayers are hindered by our wretched unbelief! We go to God and ask Him for something that is positively promised in His Word, and then we do not more than half expect to get it. "Let not that man suppose that he will receive anything from the Lord."

God who knows me, examine my heart when I come before You. Convict me of sin. That's a scary prayer. I'm always a bit afraid that You won't like what You see. How foolish that is, because You already know what I try to hide—and You love me anyway. Remove in me my selfish and limited ambition, my pride, and all those things that get in Your way. When I attempt to act as if I am the god of my life and think I know better than You do, break that self-will in me. Continue to burnish me and scrub me free of sin, that my life may reflect Your holiness in ever-increasing measure. Amen.

Great High Priest, what encouragement I gain from knowing You have gone before me. You tore down the veil that separated me from the Father after You had been tempted in every way as I am. You understand the why and provided the how of prayer. You taught us, "Let us therefore come boldly to the throne of grace, that we may. . .find grace to help in time of need" (Hebrews 4:16). Forgive me when I put other things—my family, my health, my career—in

the place that rightfully belongs to You. When
You say no, may I examine my heart to see what
drove me to prayer. Did I pray for the increase
of Your will and Kingdom, or for my own selfish
purposes? Peel the scales from my eyes that
I may see the truth. Forgive my selfishness.
Thank You for Your forgiveness and for
new beginnings. Amen.

Giving God, when I complain about what I
don't have, as if You are being stingy in Your
provision, remind me that You give with the
same measure I use to give to others. The more
I give, the more You have to press down, shake
together, and pour out until it runs over (Luke
6:38). I confess this is a tough one for me. I
never know whether I should give to the beggar
on the street—or my friend. I don't know if my
hesitation lies in a desire for their best—or to
protect myself. I have rarely given until it hurts.
Yet You gave Your only begotten Son for me, and
I still hold back? Forgive me, Lord. Open my eyes
to the needs of the foreigners, the widows and
orphans. Lead me to the right person, the right
organization, and let me open my hand
wide in response to that need. Amen.

Lord God, this chapter touched several painful
topics, and this last one is the hardest of all:
an unforgiving spirit. By Your grace, I can
and have performed acts of forgiveness. I have
prayed for enemies. I have loved them by giving
things I treasured. Those actions have taken
the edge from my feelings, but my defensive
hackles stiffen whenever they dare come close
again. I know You don't expect me to subject
myself to abuse. But You do call me to love those
who treat me spitefully, to see the best in them
instead of expecting the worst from them.
No wonder at times my prayers seem
weak, operating at quarter-power,
when I retain that spirit of unforgiveness.
Transform my heart. Amen.

CHAPTER 10:
Intercession: Every Christian's Duty, Part 1
GEORGE WHITEFIELD

*Therefore I exhort first of all that supplications,
prayers, intercessions, and giving of
thanks be made for all men.*
1 TIMOTHY 2:1

W hy is there so little love to be found
amongst Christians? Why is it the
very characteristic by which everyone should
know that we are disciples of the holy Jesus is
almost banished out of the Christian world?
We find the answer, in a great measure, owing
to a neglect or superficial performance of that
excellent part of prayer, *intercession*, or implor-
ing the divine grace and mercy in behalf of
others.

Some forget this duty of praying for others because they seldom remember to pray for
themselves. Conversely, some of those who are
constant in praying to their heavenly Father

are so selfish in their addresses to the throne of grace that they do not enlarge their petitions for the welfare of their fellow Christians as they ought. They thereby fall short of attaining that Christian charity—that unfeigned love to their brethren which their sacred profession obliges them to aspire after—and without which, though they should bestow all their goods to feed the poor and even give their bodies to be burned, yet it would profit them nothing.

Since these things are so, I shall endeavor in this discussion to show two things: First, that it is every Christian's duty to pray for others as well as for himself.

Second, whom we ought to pray for and in what manner we should do it.

First, it is every Christian's duty to pray for others as well as for himself. Prayer is a duty founded on natural religion; the very heathens never neglected it, though many Christian heathens amongst us do. It is so essential to Christianity that you might as reasonably expect to find a living man without breath as a true Christian without the spirit of prayer and supplication.

Thus, no sooner was St. Paul converted, but "behold, he is praying," said the Lord

Almighty (Acts 9:11). And thus will it be with every child of God as soon as he becomes such: prayer being truly called the natural cry of the newborn soul.

In the heart of every true believer there is a heavenly tendency, a divine attraction, which as sensibly draws him to converse with God as the lodestone attracts the needle. A deep sense of their own weakness and of Christ's fullness; a strong conviction of their natural corruption and of the necessity of renewing grace will not let them rest from crying day and night to their Almighty Redeemer, that the divine image, which they lost in Adam, may through His all-powerful mediation and the sanctifying operation of His blessed Spirit be begun, carried on, and fully perfected both in their souls and bodies.

Thus earnest, thus persistent, are all sincere Christians in praying for themselves: But then, not having so lively, lasting, and deep a sense of the wants of their Christian brethren, they are for the most part too remiss and defective in their prayers for them. Whereas, was the love of God shed abroad in our hearts and did we love our neighbor in the manner in which the Son of God our Savior loved us, and according to His command and example, we could not but be as unrelenting in our prayers for their spiritual and temporal welfare as for our own; and as earnestly desire and endeavor that others should share in the benefits of the death and passion of Jesus Christ, as we ourselves.

Let not anyone think that this is an uncommon degree of charity, a high pitch of perfection, to which not everyone can attain; for, if we are all commanded to love our neighbor (that is every man) even as ourselves—nay, to lay down our lives for the brethren—then it is the duty of all to pray for our neighbors as much as for ourselves, and by all possible acts and expressions of love and affection toward them, at all times, to show our readiness even to lay down our lives for them, if ever it should please God to call us to it.

Our blessed Savior set an example for us in that divine, that perfect and inimitable prayer recorded in the seventeenth chapter of John, which He put up just before His passion. In that prayer, we find but few petitions for His own sake, yet many for His disciples' welfare.

Likewise, in that perfect form known as the Lord's Prayer, which He has been pleased to prescribe us, we are taught to say, not *my*, but *our Father*, thereby to put us in mind, that whenever we approach the throne of grace, we ought to pray not for ourselves alone, but for all our brethren in Christ.

Intercession then is certainly a duty incumbent upon all Christians.

Second, let us consider for whom we are to intercede and how this duty is to be performed. To begin, our intercession must be *universal*. St. Paul said, "I exhort first of all that supplications, prayers, intercessions...be made for all men" (1 Tim. 2:1). For as God's mercy is over all his works, as Jesus Christ died to redeem a people out of all nations and languages, so we should pray for "all men to be saved and to come to the knowledge of the truth" (1 Tim. 2:4). Many precious promises are made in holy writ: that the gospel shall be published through the whole world, that "the earth shall be full of the knowledge of the Lord as the waters cover the sea" (Isa. 11:9). Therefore, it is our duty not to confine our petitions to our own nation, but to pray that all those nations who now sit in darkness and in the shadow of death may have the glorious gospel shine out upon them, as well as upon us. But you need not that any man should teach you this, since you yourselves are taught of God, and of Jesus Christ Himself, to pray that His kingdom may come; part of the meaning of which petition is that God's "way may be known on earth, [and His] salvation among all nations" (Ps. 67:2).

Note that the *praying for all men extends to those who rule over us*; particularly for our national leaders, and all that are put in authority under them: that we may lead quiet lives, in all godliness and honesty.

For, if we consider how heavy the burden of government is and how much the welfare of any people depends on the zeal and godly conversation of those that have the rule over them; if we set before us the many dangers and difficulties to which governors by their station are exposed, and the continual temptations they be under to luxury and self-indulgence, we shall not only pity but pray for them. Let us pray that He who preserved Esther, David, and Josiah "unspotted from the world" (James 1:27), amidst the grandeur of a court, and gave success to their designs, would also preserve them holy and unblameable and prosper all the works of their hands upon them.

We need also to *pray for those whom "the Holy Spirit has made. . .overseers, to shepherd the church of God"* (Acts 20:28).

This is what St. Paul begs, again and again, of the churches to whom he writes: In both letters to the Thessalonians, he asks them, "Brethren, pray for us" (1 Thess. 5:25; 2 Thess. 3:1), and again, in Ephesians 6:18–19, "praying always with all prayer and supplication in the Spirit. . .and for me. . .that I may open my mouth boldly to make known the mystery of the gospel." And in another place, to express his earnestness in this request, and the great importance of their prayers for him, he bids the church to "strive [or, as the original word signifies, be in agony] together with me in prayers to God for me" (Rom. 15:30). And surely, if the great St. Paul—that chosen vessel, that favorite of heaven—needed the most persistent prayers of his Christian converts, how much more do the ordinary ministers of the gospel stand in need of the intercession of their respective flocks.

I cannot but in a more especial manner insist upon this branch of your duty because it is a matter of such importance. I do not doubt that much good is frequently withheld from many, by reason of their neglecting to pray for their ministers; good which they would have received, had they prayed for them as they ought. Not to mention that people often complain of the want of diligent and faithful pastors.

But how do they deserve good pastors if they will not earnestly pray to God for such? If we will not pray to the Lord of the harvest, can it be expected He will send forth laborers into His harvest?

Besides, what ingratitude is it, not to pray for your ministers! For shall they watch and labor in the Word and doctrine for you and your salvation, and shall not you pray for them in return? If any bestow favors on your bodies, you think it right, meet, and your bounden duty to pray for them; yet shall not they be remembered in your prayers, who daily feed and nourish your souls? Add to all this that praying for your ministers will be a manifest proof of your believing, that though Paul plant, and Apollos water, yet it is God alone who gives the increase. And you will also find it the best means you can use to promote your own welfare; because God, in answer to your prayers, may impart a double portion of His Holy Spirit to them, whereby they will be qualified to deal out to you larger measures of knowledge in spiritual things and be enabled more skillfully to divide the word of truth.

Would men but constantly observe this direction, and when their ministers are praying in their name to God, humbly beseech him to perform all their petitions; or, when they are speaking in God's name to them, pray that the Holy Ghost may fall on all them that hear the word, we should find a more visible good effect of their doctrine and a greater mutual love between ministers and their people. In so doing, those ministers' hands would then be held up by the people's intercessions, and the people will never dare to vilify or traduce those who are the constant subjects of their prayers.

Next to our ministers, *our friends claim a place in our intercessions*; but then we should not content ourselves with praying in general terms for them, but suit our prayers to their particular circumstances.

When Miriam was afflicted with leprosy from God, Moses cried and said, "Please heal her, O God, I pray!" (Num. 12:13). And when the nobleman came to apply to Jesus Christ, in behalf of his child, he said, "My little daughter lies at the point of death. Come and lay Your hands on her, that she may be healed" (Mark 5:23). In like manner, when our friends are under any afflicting circumstances, we should endeavor to pray for them with a particular regard to those circumstances. For instance, is a friend sick? We should pray that if it be God's good pleasure, it may not be unto death; but if otherwise, that He would give him grace so to take his visitation, that, after this painful life ended, he may dwell with Him in life everlasting. Is a friend in doubt in an important matter? We should lay his case before God, as Moses did that of the daughters of Zelophehad (see Numbers 27), and pray that God's Holy Spirit may lead him into all truth and give all seasonable direction. Is he in want? We should pray that his faith may never fail and that in God's due time he may be relieved. And in all other cases, we should not pray for our friends only in general, but suit our petitions to their particular sufferings and afflictions; for otherwise, we may never ask perhaps for the things our friends most need.

It must be confessed that such a procedure will oblige some often to break from the forms they use; but if we accustom ourselves to it and have a deep sense of what we ask for, the most illiterate will want proper words to express themselves.

We have many noble instances in holy scripture of the success of this kind of particular intercession, but none more remarkable than that of Abraham's servant in Genesis chapter 24, who, being sent to seek a wife for Abraham's son Isaac, prayed in a most particular manner. And the sequel of the story informs us how remarkably his prayer was answered. And did Christians now pray for their friends in the same particular manner and with the same faith as Abraham's servant did for his master, they would, no doubt, in many instances, receive as visible answers and have as much reason to bless God for them, as he had.

Furthermore, just as we ought thus to

intercede for our friends, so in like manner must *we also pray for our enemies.* Jesus Himself tells us in Matthew 5:44, "Bless those who curse you... and pray for those who spitefully use you and persecute you." These commands He enforced in the strongest manner by His own example: In the very agonies and pangs of death, He prayed even for his murderers, "Father, forgive them, for they do not know what they do" (Luke 23:34). This, it must be confessed, is a difficult duty, yet not impracticable, to those who have renounced the things of this present life (from an inordinate love of which all enmities arise) and who, knowing the terrible woes denounced against those who offend Christ's little ones, can, out of real pity and a sense of their danger, pray for those by whom such offenses come.

Lastly, and to conclude this head, *we should intercede for all that are in any way afflicted* in mind, body, or estate; for all who desire and stand in need of our prayers, and for all who do not pray for themselves.

And oh! That all who hear me would set apart time every day for the due performance of this necessary duty!

Listening God, I have come to realize my prayers don't follow a set form. They don't all include adoration, confession, thanksgiving, and supplication for myself and others. It's okay if I don't always bring the needs of others before You. The problem is how seldom I do pray for others. Forgive my self-centered focus. When I promise to pray for someone, let me stop and pray for them that instant. I confess I neglect times of dedicated prayer, and that hurts not only me, but everyone I could pray for. Guide me to the means of tracking the needs of others—and teach me the discipline to maintain it and pray for them on a regular basis. Let me pray for others with the same fervor and concern with which I pray for myself. Amen.

King of kings and Lord of lords, there is no place on earth where Your Word is not heard. How humbling, how thrilling, that You call me to be a part of the spread of the Gospel to the ends of the earth. You have commanded me to make supplications, prayers, intercessions, and giving of thanks for all men (1 Timothy 2:1). Let me not pray in generalities. May I pray for specific people groups who so far have rejected the Gospel or who haven't heard. I also lift up those individuals and nations that have taken a stand against me, that they will be drawn into a saving relationship with You. That they will be transformed and blessed before You. As I pray, I rejoice that I will also be changed. Amen.

King of kings, our president and national leaders govern under Your direction, whether or not they acknowledge it. I pray that they will submit to Your authority in their lives, and that they will be people of integrity. I pray for others in leadership over us, for our pastors and overseers. That You will open doors of ministry for them. That You will be glorified through them. That they will live lives of integrity and honor. Too many religious leaders have fallen into sin. I pray both for the Bible study leaders, local pastors, and for television preachers, that they will remain faithful to You. I pray You will strengthen their families. Forgive me when I neglect to pray for my overseers. In Jesus' name, amen.

Heavenly Father, once again I come before You, asking Your forgiveness for my failure to love my brothers and sisters in Christ by praying for them. They should be easiest to remember. Their emails crowd my inbox, each heavy with grief, family emergencies, and health problems, with problems as wide-ranging as our lives. Their names appear on my church bulletin, and the pastor has updated me on their situation. Teach me first to pray for them consistently, until their need is met and the situation is resolved. Also show me how to pray for them. Eliezer made a specific request on behalf of Isaac. Open my heart to an understanding of what my friends need from You. As we pray together, we'll build each other up in faith and bring glory to Your name both in the answered prayer and in our unity. Hallelujah! Make it so, heavenly Lord. Amen.

CHAPTER 11:
Intercession: Every Christian's Duty, Part 2
GEORGE WHITEFIELD

Through the LORD's mercies we are not consumed,
because His compassions fail not.
LAMENTATIONS 3:22

Let us now look to the advantages and considerations that should excite all Christians to abound daily in this great duty of intercession.

First, intercession will fill your hearts with love for one another. He who every day heartily intercedes at the throne of grace for all mankind, cannot but in a short time be filled with love and charity to all. The frequent exercise of his love in this manner will insensibly enlarge his heart and make him partaker of that exceeding abundance of it which is in Christ Jesus our Lord! Envy, malice, revenge, and suchlike hellish tempers can never long harbor in a gracious intercessor's breast; but he will be filled with joy, peace, meekness, long-suffering, and all other graces of the Holy Spirit. By frequently laying his neighbor's wants before God, he will be touched with a fellow-feeling of them; he will rejoice with those that do rejoice, and weep with those that weep. Every blessing bestowed on others, instead of exciting envy in him, will be looked upon as an answer to his particular intercession and fill his soul with joy unspeakable and full of glory.

Abound therefore in acts of general and particular intercessions; and when you hear of your neighbor's faults, instead of relating them to and exposing them before others, lay them in secret before God and beg of Him to correct and amend them.

When you hear of a notorious sinner, instead of thinking you do well to be angry, beg of Jesus Christ to convert, and make him a monument of His free grace. You cannot imagine what a blessed alteration this practice will make in your heart, and how much you will increase day by day in the spirit of love and meekness toward all mankind!

But further, to excite you to the constant practice of this duty of intercession, consider the many instances in holy scripture of the power and efficacy of it. Great and excellent things are there recorded as the effects of this divine employ.

It has stopped plagues, it has opened and shut heaven, and it has frequently turned away God's fury from His people.

How was Abimelech's house freed from the disease God sent amongst them, at the intercession of Abraham (see Genesis 20)! When "Phinehas stood up and prayed," how soon did the plague cease! When Daniel humbled and afflicted his soul and interceded for the Lord's inheritance, how quickly was an angel dispatched to tell him, "At the beginning of your supplications the command went out" (Dan. 9:23). And, to mention but one instance more, how did God own Himself, as it were, overcome with the persistence of Moses when he was interceding for his idolatrous people? He said to Moses, "Let Me alone, that My wrath may burn hot against them and I may consume them." But Moses pleaded with the Lord for the sake of his people, and prevailed (Exodus 32).

This sufficiently shows, I could almost

say, the omnipotence of intercession, and how we may, like Jacob, wrestle with God and by a holy violence prevail both for ourselves and others. No doubt it is owing to the secret and prevailing intercessions of the few righteous souls who still remain among us, that God has yet spared this miserably sinful nation: For were there not some such faithful ones, like Moses, left to stand in the gap, we should soon be destroyed, even as was Sodom, and reduced to ashes like unto Gomorrah.

But, to stir you up yet further to this exercise of intercession, consider that in all probability, it is the frequent employment even of the glorified saints: For though they are delivered from the burden of the flesh and restored to the glorious liberty of the sons of God, yet as their happiness cannot be perfectly consummated till the resurrection of the last day when all their brethren will be glorified with them, we cannot but think they are often persistent in beseeching our heavenly Father shortly to accomplish the number of His elect and to hasten His kingdom. And shall now we, who are on earth, be often exercised in this divine employ with the glorious company of the spirits of just men made perfect? Since our happiness is so much to consist in the communion of saints in the church triumphant above, shall we not frequently intercede for the church militant here below; and earnestly beg that we may all be one, even as the Holy Jesus and His Father are one, that we may also be made perfect in one?

To provoke you to this great work and labor of love, remember that it is the never-ceasing employment of the holy and highly exalted Jesus Himself, who sits at the right hand of God, to hear all our prayers and to make continual intercession for us! Thus, he who is, on earth, constantly employed in interceding for others is also doing that which the eternal Son of God is always doing in heaven.

Imagine therefore, when you are lifting up holy hands in prayer for one another, that you see the heavens opened, and the Son of God in all His glory, as the great high priest of your salvation, is pleading for you the all-sufficient merit of His sacrifice before the throne of His heavenly Father! Join then your intercessions with His and beseech Him that they may, through Him, come up as incense and be received as a sweet-smelling savor, acceptable in the sight of God! This imagination will strengthen your faith, excite a holy earnestness in your prayers, and make you wrestle with God, as Jacob did when he saw Him face-to-face, and his life was preserved; as Abraham when he pleaded for Sodom; and as Jesus Christ Himself, when He prayed, being in an agony, so much the more earnestly the night before His bitter passion.

And now, brethren, what shall I say more, since you are taught of Jesus Christ Himself to abound in love and in this good work of praying one for another. Though ever so humble, though as poor as Lazarus, you will then become benefactors to all mankind; thousands, and twenty times ten thousands, will then be blessed for your sakes! And after you have employed a few years in this divine exercise here, you will be translated to that happy place, where you have so often wished others might be advanced; and be exalted to sit at the right hand of our all-powerful, all-prevailing Intercessor, in the kingdom of His heavenly Father hereafter.

However, I cannot but in an especial

manner press this upon you now, because all of you, amongst whom I have now been preaching, in all probability will see me no more: For I am now going (I trust under the conduct of God's most Holy Spirit) from you, knowing not what shall befall me: I need therefore your most persistent, relentless intercessions, even as St. Paul requested, that "none of these things move me; nor do I count my life dear to myself, so that I may finish my race with joy, and the ministry which I received from the Lord Jesus, to testify to the gospel of the grace of God" (Acts 20:24).

While I have been here, to the best of my knowledge, I have not failed to declare unto you the whole will of God; and though my preaching may have been a savor of death unto death to some, yet I trust it has been also a savor of life unto life to others; and therefore I earnestly hope that those will not fail to remember me in their prayers. As for my own part, the many unmerited kindnesses I have received from you will not suffer me to forget you.

Out of the deep, therefore, I trust shall my cry come unto God; and while the winds and storms are blowing over me, unto the Lord will I make my supplication for you. For it is but a little while, and we must all appear before the judgment seat of Christ, where I must give a strict account of the doctrine I have preached, and you of your improvement under it. And O, that I may never be called out as a swift witness against any of those for whose salvation I have sincerely, though too faintly, longed and labored!

It is true, I have been censured by some as acting out of sinister and selfish views, "but with me it is a very small thing that I should be judged by you or by a human court" (1 Cor. 4:3); I beseech you, brethren, by the mercies of God in Christ Jesus, pray that it may be more so! And that I may increase with the increase of grace in the knowledge and love of God through Jesus Christ our Lord.

And now, brethren, what shall I say more? I could wish to continue my discourse much longer, for I can never fully express the desire of my soul toward you! Yet I say with St. Paul, "Finally, brethren, whatever things are true, whatever things are noble, whatever things are just, whatever things are pure, whatever things are lovely, whatever things are of good report, if there is any virtue and if there is anything praiseworthy" (Phil. 4:8); "if there is any consolation in Christ, if any comfort of love, if any fellowship of the Spirit, if any affection and mercy" (Phil. 2:1), meditate on these things, and of those which your pastors have declared and will yet declare unto you; and continue under their ministry to "work out your own salvation with fear and trembling" (Phil. 2:12) so that whether I should never see you anymore, or whether it shall please God to bring me back again at any time, I may always have the satisfaction of knowing that your conversation is such as is "worthy of the gospel of Christ" (Phil. 1:27).

I almost persuade myself that I could willingly suffer all things, so that it might in any ways promote the salvation of your precious and immortal souls. I beseech you, as my last request, to "remember those who rule over you" in the Lord (Heb. 13:7), and be always ready to attend on their ministry, as it is your bounden duty. Think not that I desire to have myself exalted at the expense of another's character, but rather think this: Not to have any man's person too much in admiration, but esteem all your ministers highly in love, as they justly deserve for their work's sake.

And now, "brethren, I commend you to God and to the word of His grace, which is able to build you up and give you an inheritance among all those who are sanctified" (Acts 20:32). May God reward you for all your works of faith and labors of love and make you to abound more and more in every good word and work toward all men. May He truly convert all that have been convinced and awaken all that are dead in trespasses and sins! May He confirm all that are wavering! And may you all go on from one degree of grace unto another, till you arrive unto the measure of the stature of the fullness of Christ; and thereby be made meet to stand before that God in whose "presence is fullness of joy; [and at whose] right hand are pleasures forevermore" (Ps. 16:11). Amen! Amen!

*Our Father, make Your people one in prayer.
You have commanded me to rejoice with those
who rejoice, and instead I struggle with envy.
I compare my struggles to their good news, and
wonder why You have favored them. Or when
they need me to weep with them, I may inwardly
gloat, thinking they won't be so quick to judge
another time. Forgive me. Let me set aside that
selfish ambition. Increase my understanding of
how Your body, the church, works. You are our
Head, so that we function as one. I thank You
that You bless me when You bless them. Open my
spirit that their suffering becomes my suffering.
How I thank You that through prayer,
we can seek to be one in love, as You
have commanded us. Amen.*

*Lord God, how often we corporately cry out,
"God bless America," but fail to acknowledge
You where it counts. How thankful I am for
those who remain faithful to You in my beloved
country. Every new generation contains a few
who do not recognize their heritage, Your image
in the pattern of our history, both of the nation*

and of families. Let that not be so in my family,
in my generation. Although I am only one
woman, I am one. May I be found faithful on
the day You weigh America. I pray that You will
raise up believers, at home and abroad, to bring
the needs of peoples and nations before You.
In Jesus' name, amen.

Our heavenly Father, You gave us one Lord, one
faith, one baptism, when You called us to one hope
(Ephesians 4:4–5). I confess that at times I am like
Euodia and Syntyche, who brought trouble to the
Philippian church and allowed division to sneak
in and disrupt, whether in personality conflicts
or differing theologies (Philippians 4:2). Where
should I draw the line between accepting differing
interpretations and false doctrine? I confess it's
easier to worship with people with similar tastes.
I may be comfortable with the rhythms of liturgy
. . .or I may want the freedom to raise my arms
and dance. I look forward to heaven, when we all
worship as one, our only concern to glorify the name
of our Lord Jesus Christ. Until then, remove any
stumbling blocks of unforgiveness from among us,
that our loving unity will testify to Your
presence among us. Amen.

Omnipotent and Omnipresent God, too often my myopic vision sees only the concerns of those in my immediate vicinity. I willingly limit my world to my family, my job, my living situation, whereas my prayers can reach the billions of people upon the earth and beyond my death. Operate on my spiritual eyes that I may see. Remove the earthly concerns that clog the arteries of my heart. Cleanse me, prepare me, to bring the needs of a hurting world before You. Teach me the faith to pray for what I will not see with my own eyes or in my lifetime. Give me a desire to pray for those who otherwise have no one to pray for them. I thank You for the awesome power and opportunity prayer affords. Amen.

CHAPTER 12:
Answered Prayer
E. M. BOUNDS

*"If you abide in Me, and My words abide
in you, you will ask what you desire,
and it shall be done for you."*
JOHN 15:7

It is answered prayer which brings praying out of the realm of dry, dead things, and makes praying a thing of life and power. It is the answer to prayer which brings things to pass, changes the natural trend of things, and orders all things according to the will of God. It is the answer to prayer which takes praying out of the regions of fanaticism and saves it from being utopian or from being merely fanciful. It is the answer to prayer which makes praying a power for God and also for man. It makes praying real and divine. Unanswered prayers are training schools for unbelief, an imposition and a nuisance, an impertinence to God and to man.

Answers to prayer are the only surety that we have prayed aright. What marvelous power there is in prayer! What untold miracles it works in this world! What untold benefits to men does it secure to those who pray! Why is it that the average prayer by the million goes begging for an answer?

The millions of unanswered prayers are not to be solved by the mystery of God's will. We are not the sport of His sovereign power. He is not playing at "make-believe" in His marvelous promises to answer prayer. The whole explanation is found in our wrong praying. We "ask and do not receive, because [we] ask amiss" (James 4:3). If all unanswered prayers were dumped into the ocean, they would come very near to filling it. Child of God, can you pray? Are your prayers answered? If not, why not? Answered prayer is the proof of your real praying.

The efficacy of prayer from a Bible standpoint lies solely in the answer to prayer. The benefit of prayer has been well and popularly maximized by the saying, "It moves the arm which moves the universe." To get unquestioned answers to prayer is not only important as to the satisfying of our desires, but is the evidence of our abiding in Christ. It becomes more important still. The mere act of praying is no test of our relation to God. The act of praying may be a real dead performance. It may be the routine of habit. But to pray and receive clear answers, not once or twice, but daily, this is the sure test, and is the gracious point of our vital connection with Jesus Christ.

Read again our Lord's words in this connection: "If you abide in Me, and My words abide in you, you will ask what you desire, and it shall be done for you." To God and to man, the answer to prayer is the all-important part of our praying. The answer to prayer, direct and unmistakable, is the evidence of God's being. It proves that God lives, that there is a God, an intelligent Being who is interested in His creatures, and who listens to them when they approach Him in prayer. There is no proof so clear and demonstrative that God exists than prayer and its answer. This was Elijah's plea: "Hear me, O Lord, hear me, that this people may know that You are the Lord God" (1 Kings 18:37).

The answer to prayer is the part of prayer which glorifies God. Unanswered prayers are dumb oracles which leave the praying ones in darkness, doubt, and bewilderment and which carry no conviction to the unbeliever. It is not the act or the attitude of praying which gives efficacy to prayer. It is not abject prostration of the body before God, the vehement or quiet utterance to God, nor the exquisite beauty and poetry of the diction of our prayers which does the deed. It is not the marvelous array of argument and eloquence in praying which makes prayer effectual. Not one or all of these are the things which glorify God. It is the *answer* which brings glory to His Name.

Elijah might have prayed on Carmel's heights till this good day with all the fire and energy of his soul, and if no answer had been given, no glory would have come to God. Peter might have shut himself up with Dorcas's dead body till he himself died on his knees, and if no answer had come, no glory to God nor good to man would have followed, but only doubt, blight, and dismay.

Answer to prayer is the convincing proof

of our right relations to God. Jesus said at the grave of Lazarus: "Father, I thank You that You have heard Me. And I know that You always hear Me, but because of the people who are standing by I said this, that they may believe that You sent Me" (John 11:41–42). The answer of His prayer was the proof of His mission from God, as the answer to Elijah's prayer was made to the woman whose son he raised to life. She said, "Now by this I know that you are a man of God" (1 Kings 17:24). He is highest in the favor of God who has the readiest access and the greatest number of answers to prayer from Almighty God.

Prayer ascends to God by an invariable law, even by more than law: by the will, the promise, and the presence of a personal God. The answer comes back to earth by all the promise, the truth, the power, and the love of God.

Not to be concerned about the answer to prayer is not to pray. What a world of waste there is in praying. What myriads of prayers have been offered for which no answer is returned, no answer is longed for, and no answer is expected! We have been nurturing a false faith and hiding the shame of our loss and inability to pray by the false, comforting plea that God does not answer directly or objectively, but indirectly and subjectively. We have persuaded ourselves that by some kind of hocus-pocus of which we are wholly unconscious in its process and its results, we have been made better.

Conscious that God has not answered us directly, we have solaced ourselves with the delusive unction that God has in some impalpable way, and with unknown results, given us something better. Or we have comforted and nurtured our spiritual sloth by saying that it is not God's will to give it to us. Faith teaches God's praying ones that it is God's will to answer prayer. God answers all prayers and every prayer of His true children who truly pray.

> Prayer makes the darkened cloud withdraw,
> Prayer climbs the ladder Jacob saw;
> Gives exercise to faith and love,
> Brings every blessing from above.

The emphasis in the scripture is always given to the answer to prayer. All things from God are given in answer to prayer. God Himself, His presence, His gifts, and His grace, one and all, are secured by prayer. The medium by which God communicates with men is prayer. The most real thing in prayer, its very essential end, is the answer it secures. The mere repetition of words in prayer, the counting of beads, the multiplying mere words of prayer as works of supererogation as if there was virtue in the number of prayers to avail, is a vain delusion, an empty thing, a useless service. Prayer looks directly to securing an answer. This is its design. It has no other end in view.

Communion with God, of course, is in prayer. There is sweet fellowship there with our God through His Holy Spirit. Enjoyment of God there is in praying—sweet, rich, and strong. The graces of the Spirit in the inner soul are nurtured by prayer, kept alive and promoted in their growth by this spiritual exercise. But not one or all of these benefits of prayer have in them the essential end of prayer. The divinely appointed channel through which all good and all grace flow to our souls and bodies is prayer.

Prayer is appointed to convey
The blessings God designs to give.

Prayer is divinely ordained as the means by which all temporal and spiritual good is gained to us. Prayer is not an end in itself. It is not something done to be rested in, something we have done, about which we are to congratulate ourselves. It is a means to an end. It is something we do which brings us something in return, without which the praying is valueless. Prayer always aims at securing an answer.

We are rich and strong, good and holy, beneficent and benignant, by answered prayer. It is not the mere performance, the attitude, nor the words of prayer which bring benefit to us, but it is the answer sent direct from heaven. Conscious, real answers to prayer bring real good to us. This is not praying merely for self, or simply for selfish ends. The selfish character cannot exist when the prayer conditions are fulfilled.

It is by these answered prayers that human nature is enriched. The answered prayer brings us into constant and conscious communion with God, awakens and enlarges gratitude, and excites the melody and lofty inspiration of praise. Answered prayer is the mark of God in our praying. It is the exchange with heaven, and it establishes and realizes a relationship with the unseen. We give our prayers in exchange for the divine blessing. God accepts our prayers through the atoning blood and gives Himself, His presence, and His grace in return.

All holy affections are affected by answered prayers. By the answers to prayer all holy principles are matured, and faith, love, and hope have their enrichment by answered prayer. The answer is found in all true praying. The answer is in prayer strongly as an aim, a desire expressed, and its expectation and realization give persistence and realization to prayer. It is the fact of the answer which makes the prayer and which enters into its very being. To seek no answer to prayer takes the desire, the aim, and the heart out of prayer. It makes praying a dead, stockish thing, fit only for dumb idols. It is the answer which brings praying into Bible regions and makes it a desire realized, a pursuit, an interest; which clothes it with flesh and blood, and makes it a prayer, throbbing with all the true life of prayer, affluent with all the paternal relations of giving and receiving, of asking and answering.

God holds all good in His own hands. That good comes to us through our Lord Jesus Christ because of His all-atoning merits, by asking it in His name. The sole command in which all the others of its class belong is "Ask. . .seek. . . knock." And the sole promise is its counterpart, its necessary equivalent and results: "It will be given. . .you will find. . .it will be opened to you" (Matt. 7:7).

God is so much involved in prayer and its hearing and answering, that all of His attributes and His whole being are centered in that great fact. It distinguishes Him as peculiarly beneficent, wonderfully good, and powerfully attractive in His nature. "O You who hear prayer, to You all flesh will come" (Ps. 65:2).

Faithful, O Lord, Thy mercies are
A rock that cannot move;
A thousand promises declare
Thy constancy of love.

Not only does the Word of God stand surety for the answer to prayer, but all the attributes of God conspire to the same end. God's veracity is at stake in the engagements to answer prayer. His wisdom, His truthfulness, and His goodness are involved. God's infinite and inflexible rectitude is pledged to the great end of answering the prayers of those who call upon Him in time of need. Justice and mercy blend into oneness to secure the answer to prayer. It is significant that the very justice of God comes into play and stands hard by God's faithfulness in the strong promise He makes of the pardon of sins and of cleansing from sin's pollutions: "If we confess our sins, He is faithful and just to forgive us our sins and to cleanse us from all unrighteousness" (1 John 1:9). God's kingly relation to man, with all of its authority, unites with the fatherly relation and with all of its tenderness to secure the answer to prayer.

Our Lord Jesus Christ is most fully committed to the answer of prayer. He promises, "Whatever you ask in My name, that I will do, that the Father may be glorified in the Son"

(John 14:13). How well assured the answer to prayer is, when that answer is to glorify God the Father! And how eager Jesus Christ is to glorify His Father in heaven! So eager is He to answer prayer which always and everywhere brings glory to the Father that no prayer offered in His name is denied or overlooked by Him. Says our Lord Jesus Christ again, giving fresh assurance to our faith, "If you ask anything in My name, I will do it" (John 14:14). So says He once more, "Ask what you desire, and it shall be done for you" (John 15:7).

Come, my soul, thy suit prepare,
Jesus loves to answer prayer;
He Himself has bid thee pray,
Therefore will not say thee nay.

*Lord God, I give thanks for the prayers You
have answered beyond what I could imagine
to the glory of Your name. How I rejoice
when Your name is made holy in answering
my prayers. You are the God of Wonders. You
delight in doing what only You can do. You can
remove the cancerous cells, and You can bring
the one battling cancer safely home to You. You
can also arrange the timing of an encouraging
phone call. You are Lord of all, working in
and through everything around me to answer
prayer. Thank You for teaching me more about
You with every answer, filling in a little more
of the infinite picture that is You. Amen.*

*Great High Priest, how grateful I am that You
understand my human frailty. I confess there
are times that my prayers are little more than
a gesture, when I don't feel Your presence or
hear Your voice and doubt You are listening.
And yet You answer! May I never think of
prayer as fanciful, a vain repetition of words.
Through the rhythm of my prayers and Your
answers, You show me prayer is practical and*

necessary and above all real. I thank You
not only for providing for my needs, but also
for demonstrating that prayer works. May
answers to prayer encourage me to pray more
and more boldly. In Jesus' name, amen.

Guiding God, what better proof do I need that
I am on the right path than Your answered
prayer? How I rejoice when doors fly open
before I knock. Enlarge my steps in the light of
answered prayer, that I may eagerly run the race
You have set before me, assured that I will finish.
Those answered prayers build my faith, hope,
and love. And how I need that encouragement
for those times when Your answers are slow
in coming, when I have no clear direction. If I
always have clear skies ahead, how will I know
how to act when storms come? I choose to rejoice
both on sunny days and storm days. Your answers
will be all the sweeter after the storm. Amen.

Lord God, how is it possible that the God of the
universe has called me friend (John 15:15)?
And as my friend, You want to talk with me
often. You want to hear about the events of my
day, everything from the pleasure of hot water
in the shower to the disappointment when the

power goes out during my favorite TV show.
And You desire to impart to me Your heartbeat,
the concerns on Your heart. Make me as eager to
spend time with You as You are to speak with me.
Forgive me when I treat prayer as an item on
my to-do list. Make it an attitude of the heart.
Beyond all that prayer can and will accomplish,
it's all about You, the heart of worship. Amen.

If You Liked This Book, Check Out...

1,001 Prayers to Energize Your Prayer Life
Prayer is a powerful privilege given to Christians, but we often struggle to know where to start. Here, readers will find hundreds of uplifting and challenging prayer starters in *1,001 Prayers to Energize Your Prayer Life*. This compact book offers simple, heartfelt prayers for many of life's situations, and readers will find just the right pick-me-up for daily conversations with their heavenly Father.

Paperback / 978-1-68322-345-0 / $5.99

Prayers with Purpose for Women
This practical and powerful prayer guide helps women begin or end their days by offering specific prayer starters for 21 key areas of life. Topical chapters include emotions, home, health, work, finances, career, and family and are complemented by relevant scripture selections.

Paperback / 978-1-61626-869-5 / $4.99